LITTLe CrocHeT

LITTLE CROCHET

modern designs for babies and toddlers

Linda Permann

POTTER
CRAFT

NEW YORK

This book is dedicated to my nephew, Tegue,

for reminding me what's important in life. I am
having so much fun watching you grow, and I hope we
always make time to laugh and play together.

Published in the United States by Potter Craft, an imprint of the Crown Publishing Group, a division of Random House, Inc., New York.

www.crownpublishing.com

www.pottercraft.com

POTTER CRAFT and colophon is a registered trademark of Random House, Inc.

Library of Congress Cataloging-in-Publication Data

Permann, Linda.

  Little crochet : modern designs for babies and toddlers / Linda Permann. — 1st ed.

     p. cm.

  Includes index.

  ISBN 978-0-307-58658-2

  1. Crocheting—Patterns. 2. Infants' clothing. 3. Infants' supplies. I. Title.

  TT825.P395 2010

  746.43'4—dc22

                           2010017781

Printed in China

Design by woolypear

Photography by Heather Weston

Illustrations copyright © 2011 by woolypear

Tech Editing and Schematics by Kj Hay

Crochet Diagrams by Karen Manthey

Thanks to the Craft Yarn Council of America (www.yarnstandards.com) for their Standard Yarn Weight System chart, which appears on page 19.

10 9 8 7 6 5 4 3 2 1

First Edition

contents

1

BEFORE YOU BEGIN 14

2

LITTLE NURSERY 28

Felted Play Rug 54

3
LITTLe
CLOTHes 58

Boat Neck
Sweater 60

Sweet Daisy
Sundress 64

Cozy Crawlers
Leg Warmers 68

Striped Yoke
Cardigan 72

Sock It to Me
Sweater Vest 76

Strawberry Patch
Party Frock 82

Cutie Patootie
Pants 88

4
LITTLE
GIFTS 112

introduction

One of the first handmade gifts I gave in my adult life was a crocheted baby blanket made for my friend Petra's new baby. I was still a new crocheter at the time, just out of college and working as a temp in New York City. I worked on the blanket for several weeks, making it with fluffy pastel yarn and simple double crochet stitches. On the day of the baby shower, I tied the blanket up with a pretty ribbon and rode the train from Queens to Manhattan's Upper West Side. The shower was a ritzy affair to the down-home Texas girl I was at the time, and when Petra began to open the presents, she unwrapped a dazzling silver rattle from Tiffany, a colorful baby play set, and—most worrying to me—a really gorgeous blanket from Neiman Marcus. I became nervous about my handmade blanket, and fantasized about sneaking out of the party so I could give Petra a better gift later. But when she opened my present, she and the guests oohed and ahhed. All of the gifts were beautiful, but mine was unique and crocheted with love.

In the years since that baby shower I've made innumerable items for new babies and their big brothers and sisters. But my interest in making things for kids really took off when my sister was expecting her first baby, a little boy she named Tegue. I couldn't wait to crochet for him, but I wasn't able to find many patterns that appealed to me. I love to play with the full range of colors, fibers, and yarn weights available today—and I was ready to explore designs that went beyond pastel, worsted-weight acrylic yarn. I knew it was up to me to create the patterns I wanted to use, so I started to design my own set of clothes, toys, and accessories for my nephew. As with the embellishments in my first book, *Crochet Adorned,* I found that I couldn't resist the small scale of the designs—I thrive on projects that are quick to complete. Suddenly, I realized what my next book would be about. *Little Crochet* is my collection of patterns for today's crocheters and the little ones they love.

You may have picked up this book because there's a new baby in your life, or perhaps you need fresh patterns for a favorite little friend. Maybe you're new to crochet and you want to try out some small projects to practice your stitches. You're in the right place. The projects in this book are fun to make but not overly complicated. You'll find patterns for every skill level, from easy ideas perfect for beginners (or last-minute gifts) to more challenging patterns that yield heirloom-quality results.

For accessories, baby care items, and toys, turn to Little Nursery (Chapter 2, page 28) and Little Gifts (Chapter 4, page 112). These chapters contain colorful projects that are practical and fun and include many great one-size-fits-all gifts for kids of any age. The garments in Little Clothes (Chapter 3, page 58) have a classic feel that boys and girls will love to wear—and you'll be able to make them again and again as the children in your life grow. Most patterns include sizes to fit babies from 4 weeks to 4 years old. In some cases the patterns can be adapted further to accommodate older children simply by using heavier yarn and larger hooks.

I hope you'll use the patterns in this book as an opportunity to play with color, texture, and new-to-you techniques. I've chosen modern, sophisticated colors and peppered the book with suggestions for using alternate palettes and striping techniques in order to make the most of each pattern. But before you raise your hook, turn to Chapter 1 (page 14) for help choosing tools and yarn and for explanations of the patterns and symbol diagrams included in this book. The Appendix (page 146) at the back of the book contains an in-depth refresher course on basic and advanced stitches, along with useful finishing techniques. Ideas for crafty touches, such as embroidery, sewing, and appliqué, are sprinkled throughout. I think that finishing touches can turn even the simplest crochet into something special to be passed down through generations.

Here's to many years of colorful crochet for you and the little ones in your life!

Happy Crocheting!

Linda Permann
www.lindamade.com

P.S. I'd love to see what you make! Upload your projects by pattern name to www.ravelry.com or drop me a line through my website, www.lindamade.com.

1

BEFORE
YOU BEGIN

TOOLS

Working with the right tools will make crocheting for your little one a pleasure! If you're new to crocheting, try different combinations of yarn and hooks to discover your preferences. I also encourage you to venture outside of the craft store aisles and visit your local yarn shop for supplies. Your crocheted gifts are sure to be passed down to siblings or cousins and treasured for years to come, so high-quality fibers are worth the investment.

Hooks

Crochet hooks come in many shapes, sizes, and materials, including aluminum, steel, bamboo, hardwoods, glass, and even bone. I recommend aluminum hooks for beginners, but within that category there are many differences between brands of hooks, such as the shape of the tip and the size of the handle. Try a few different styles to see what you like.

Hooks come in a range of diameters, which are measured in millimeters. Generally, you'll use a smaller hook with a thin yarn and a larger hook with a bulky yarn. Hooks come in letter sizes that are somewhat standardized, but always measure the **millimeter size** of your hook in order to match the recommended hook size for a pattern in this book, as there are known discrepancies between hook manufacturers. Despite the industry's efforts to standardize hook size, some hooks have the same letter name but a different metric size, or have a metric size that doesn't correspond to a letter size at all. For this reason, use the chart at right as a general guideline to available hook sizes, but know that you may find real-world discrepancies. To double check the diameter of your hook, insert the shaft (the straight area between the hook and the thumb grip) into the holes on a knit gauge (Additional

Supplies, page 19)—until you find one that fits your hook. The millimeter measurement listed above the hole is equal to the diameter of your hook.

HOOK SIZES

US SIZE	METRIC SIZE	US SIZE	METRIC SIZE
B-1	2.25 mm	J-10	6 mm
C-2	2.75 mm	K-10½	6.5 mm
D-3	3.25 mm	L-11	8 mm
E-4	3.5 mm	M/N-13	9mm
F-5	3.75 mm	N/P-15	10mm
G-6	4 mm	P/Q	15 mm
7	4.5 mm	Q	16 mm
H-8	5mm	S	19 mm
I-9	5.5 mm		

for moms and dads to care for the baby's handmade garments and ensure that they're worn often. Easy-to-find washable yarns include cotton, superwash wool, and acrylic. And here's a secret: Sometimes you can ignore the label and try machine washing a "hand wash only" yarn—just be sure to crochet, then wash, a swatch of the yarn before you commit to buying all of the yarn for the project. Many organic cottons and synthetic blends will survive a trip through the gentle cycle unscathed. Never machine wash 100 percent wool yarn unless the label recommends it, otherwise the yarn will shrink and felt.

I've chosen natural fibers for most of the patterns in this book. I really enjoy working with cottons and wools—they come in great colors and are breathable and soft, making them perfect for babies with sensitive skin. However, if you prefer different fibers, feel free to substitute yarn as necessary—buy the yarn that makes sense for you, your little one, and your budget.

Yarn

An amazing array of fiber options exist for today's crocheter. If you have a local yarn shop, I encourage you to take a field trip to explore the yarn available to you—mine sells yarn made not only from wool, alpaca, acrylic, and cotton, but also camel, bison, yak, milk fibers, sugar cane, banana plants, and bamboo! Since projects for kids are small, they're the perfect opportunity to try out a new fiber or splurge on a little luxurious yarn. If you've never been to your local yarn shop before, you might be surprised at how affordable some of their fibers are.

When choosing yarn for babies and toddlers, the main characteristics to look for are durability and washability. Some parents, especially those who knit or crochet, may enjoy receiving luxurious hand-wash-only items, but realistically, they'll have their hands full when the baby arrives. Machine-washable (and -dryable) fibers will make it easy

FOR THE LOVE OF SOCK YARN!

If you've always loved the variety of colors and dye patterns available in sock yarns, but aren't much of a sock knitter, you're in luck! Sock yarn is perfectly suited for making kids' clothing—after all, it is designed to be durable and washable. The thinner weight of sock yarn flatters small bodies and creates a much more wearable fabric than many bulky and worsted-weight yarns. Plus, sock yarns are sold in large skeins—some contain as many as 450 yards (412m). That's enough yarn to crochet a baby's sweater vest (Sock It to Me Sweater Vest, page 76)! Although you might think of sock yarn as expensive, try doing a cost-per-yard price comparison. One ball of sock yarn often contains the equivalent yardage of anywhere from 2–4 skeins of other yarns.

single crochet over a 4" (10cm) square. Choose an alternative yarn with similar fiber content and the same weight category as the suggested yarn to ensure that you will be able to match the gauge given in the pattern (Gauge, page 24).

HOW MUCH YARN?

When you're substituting yarns, you'll also need to do a quick calculation to find out how many balls of yarn to buy. Just divide the yards needed to complete the project by the yards per ball of yarn. For instance, if the pattern calls for 200 yards (184m) of yarn and the yarn you're using comes in 92-yard (84m) skeins, here's how you would do the math:

$$\frac{200 \text{ yards (184m) needed}}{92 \text{ yards (84m) per ball of yarn}} = 2.17 \text{ balls needed}$$

In this example, you would need to buy 3 balls of the yarn to make the project. **Always buy enough yarn to finish your project.** Most yarn stores have exchange policies that will allow you to return any unused yarn, and it's much easier to buy and return one extra ball of yarn than to come back to the shop when your project is almost finished, only to find that they have sold out of the color or dye lot you need.

> TIP Many yarn companies do not include crochet gauge information on yarn labels, so you might find it easier to compare the recommended knitting gauges instead. Consult the chart to find the weight category of the featured yarn, and compare the knitting gauge for that weight category to the knitting gauge on the label of the yarn you wish to substitute.

Substituting Yarn

I've used some of my favorite yarns for the patterns in this book, but you might not be able to find all of them in your area. The availability of yarns and colorways is always changing, and on top of that, you may not like the color or the price of the yarn I chose. Perhaps you're worried that the baby will be allergic to wool, or you want to use a more luxurious yarn than I picked. All of these are great reasons to try the pattern with a different yarn!

To make yarn substitutions less daunting, I've included the yardage and fiber content of the yarn shown in each pattern as well as an icon with the general weight category (see the chart opposite for explanations) of the yarn. This number category will give you gauge information—that is, how many stitches and rows you *should* be able to work in

YARN WEIGHT SYMBOL & CATEGORY NAMES	0 LACE	1 SUPER FINE	2 FINE	3 LIGHT	4 MEDIUM	5 BULKY	6 SUPER BULKY
TYPE OF YARNS IN CATEGORY	Fingering, 10-count crochet thread	Sock, Fingering, Baby	Sport, Baby	DK, Light Worsted	Worsted, Afghan, Aran	Chunky, Craft, Rug	Bulky, Roving
KNIT GAUGE RANGE* IN STOCKINETTE STITCH TO 4 INCHES	33–40** sts	27–32 sts	23–26 sts	21–24 st	16–20 sts	12–15 sts	6–11 sts
CROCHET GAUGE* RANGES IN SINGLE CROCHET TO 4 INCHES	32–42 double crochets**	21–32 sts	16–20 sts	12–17 sts	11–14 sts	8–11 sts	5–9 sts
RECOMMENDED HOOK IN METRIC SIZE RANGE	Steel*** 1.6–1.4mm	2.25–3.5mm	3.5–4.5mm	4.5–5.5mm	5.5–6.5mm	6.5–9mm	9mm and larger
RECOMMENDED HOOK IN U.S. SIZE RANGE	Steel*** 6, 7, 8 Regular hook B–1	B–1 to E–4	E–4 to 7	7 to I–9	I–9 to K–10½	K–10½ to M–13	M–13 and larger

* GUIDELINES ONLY: The above reflect the most commonly used gauges and needle or hook sizes for specific yarn categories.

** Lace weight yarns are usually knitted or crocheted on larger needles and hooks to create lacy, openwork patterns. Accordingly, a gauge range is difficult to determine. Always follow the gauge stated in your pattern.

*** Steel crochet hooks are sized differently from regular hooks—the higher the number, the smaller the hook, which is the reverse of regular hook sizing.

organic Fibers

When you're choosing yarn, you'll probably notice more and more fibers labeled "organic." Although these yarns are more expensive, many parents choose them because fewer chemicals are used in the production and processing of the yarn, which is good for the earth—and for babies. Organic yarns are available in a range of natural colors, and some are dyed with non-toxic, natural dyes.

If your budget allows, consider organic yarn for items that will be close to baby's skin, such as washcloths, blankets, and soakers, or when you'd like to crochet with cotton, a crop whose production is known to be pesticide intensive. You may want to research yarns before buying them to see what different organic labels mean. And keep in mind that "natural" does not always mean organic. Many yarns derived from natural sources, such as sugar cane and bamboo, are made by chemical processes that turn the fiber into viscose. Examine the fiber content listed on the label, rather than the name of the yarn, to be sure of what you are buying. For yarn that has been certified organic from production through processing, choose labels that clearly state the yarn is organic.

Additional Supplies

These tools will complete your kit and make crocheting a snap!

Yarn needles: Choose large-eyed blunt needles that won't split your yarn. I like needles with a bent tip—they make it easy to work yarn tails through stitches when seaming or weaving in ends.

Stitch markers: Look for clasping or split-ring type stitch markers—you need to be able to move them around your work. Safety pins or scraps of yarn will do in a pinch.

Knit gauge: This handy tool makes it easy to measure your gauge swatch to ensure that you have the correct tension before you start a project. You can use the holes in the gauge to measure the size of any unlabeled crochet hooks.

T-pins, spray bottle, and blocking board: To block your work, you'll need rust-proof, sturdy pins (available inexpensively at office supply stores), a spray bottle filled with water, and a soft surface to spread out your work and pin it in place. For more information on blocking, turn to page 153.

Scissors: Little snips make it easy to trim yarn tails. Be sure to store them with your tools and use them only on yarn to keep the blades sharp.

Buttons, ribbons, and other embellishments: These finishing touches will make your projects stand out.

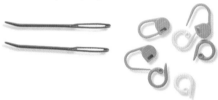

BUTTONS, RIBBONS, AND POM-POMS: OH MY!

Babies love to put things in their mouths, so it's important to ensure that any buttons, ribbons, and embellishments are securely sewn on crocheted garments and toys. As a general rule, any item that fits through a cardboard toilet paper tube is considered a choking hazard for children under three. Please be sure to check garments for loose buttons and ribbons each time you launder them. If you give a gift that includes these details, gently remind the parents to check them often. Most of the patterns in this book are written with extra-large neck openings to pull over children's heads with ease, and any buttonhole bands are worked into the edging separately from the main pieces of the garments—you can skip the band entirely if you prefer.

pattern essentials

Part of the fun of crocheting for kids is not having to worry too much

about differently shaped bodies. But sizing and fit are still important.

A few inches in size can mean months of development for babies

and toddlers, so be sure not to skip over any of the steps you would

follow with adult-sized garments. Careful attention to gauge is

especially important.

If you are new to crochet, don't be intimidated by the row-by-row instructions. In the following pages, you'll find a complete list of abbreviations used, as well as guidelines for understanding visual guides like diagrams and schematics. Crochet basics and more advanced stitches and techniques can be found in the Appendix, page 146.

Choosing a Size: Making Garments That Fit Your Baby

Each of the garments in this book is sized to fit a range of ages, but realistically, there is no such thing as a standard size for babies and toddlers. Finished measurements for each garment are listed in the pattern instructions along with a suggested age range, but you should choose which "age" size to make based on the actual measurements of the intended recipient. If you are making a garment for a child who's already been born, it's best to measure them and compare their body measurements to the finished size of the garment. Major measurements, such as chest and length, are given at the beginning of each pattern—refer to the schematic (see page 27) to check other measurements. The illustration at right shows the critical areas to consider when taking and comparing measurements. The child's chest circumference should be at least 2–4"

(5–10cm) smaller than the finished garment. If you still aren't sure which size to pick, measure the clothes that fit the child well and use those measurements as a guideline. If the intended recipient doesn't live nearby, ask what size he or she wears and take a guess based on that information. If the child is between sizes, crochet the larger size.

When making garments for a baby that hasn't been born yet, consider the due date and how old the child will be when the garment is in season. For instance, if the baby is due in November and you want to make them a warm wool sweater, the 0–6 months size would probably fit well during their first year. But if the baby is due in April, it might be December before they'll get a lot of use out of a wool sweater, so the 6–12 months size would be more appropriate. Keep in mind that some babies will never fit into the smallest size of clothing, and some may take months to grow into it. If you are not sure which size to choose, make the bigger size to give the baby room to grow. The garments in this book are designed so that, ideally, they'll still fit the older end of the given age range. That is, a garment sized at 0–6 months should fit a baby until he or she is 6 months old, meaning that it may be quite large on a newborn.

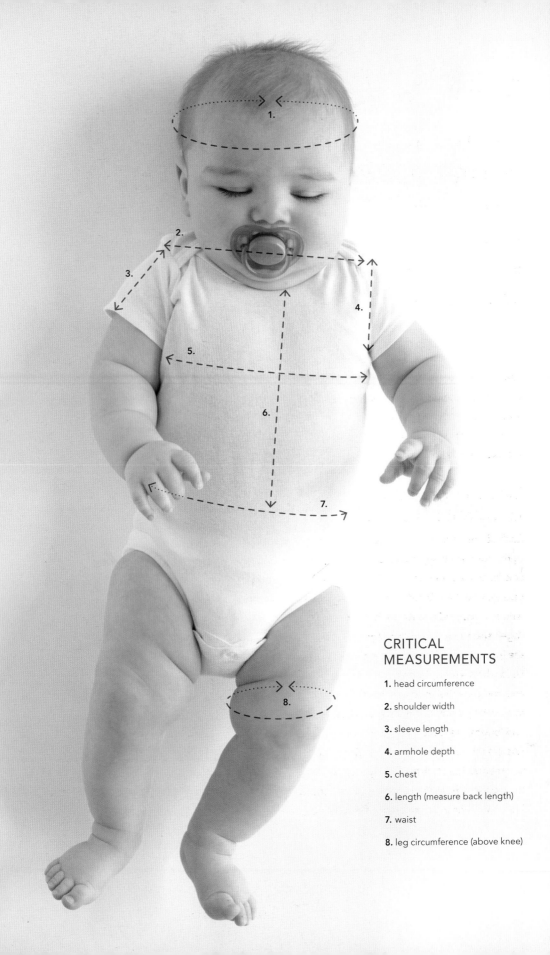

CRITICAL
MEASUREMENTS

1. head circumference

2. shoulder width

3. sleeve length

4. armhole depth

5. chest

6. length (measure back length)

7. waist

8. leg circumference (above knee)

When following a pattern with multiple sizes, directions for all of the sizes are combined into one pattern. Instruction for the smallest size appears first, with subsequent sizes in parenthesis. For a project that can be crocheted in sizes **0–6 months (6–12 months, 12–18 months, 2 years, 4 years)**, for example, a pattern might say: **Row 4:** Ch 3, **dc in next 6 (7, 8, 9, 10) dc,** 2 dc in next st. To make the 2 years size, you would dc in next 9 dc; to make the 4 years size, you would dc in next 10 dc, and so on.

The easiest way to keep all of these numbers straight is to make a photocopy of the pattern and circle or highlight the numbers that correspond to your size throughout the pattern. Do this before you begin crocheting.

Gauge

When making clothes for babies and toddlers, it's especially important to ensure you are crocheting at the listed gauge. Gauge, or tension, refers to how tightly or loosely the yarn is crocheted, and it is measured by the number of stitches and rows in a certain area of fabric. Being off by even ¼" (6mm) in gauge can make a difference of several inches in the size of a finished garment, and those few inches represent a jump of several months in age-size for small children.

To make a gauge swatch, crochet a piece of fabric at least 4" (10cm) square in the listed stitch pattern. Wash and block the swatch in the same way as you intend to wash and block the finished item. Count the number of stitches and rows in a 4" (10cm) area of your swatch (for instance, 20 stitches worked over 18 rows) and compare them to the gauge listed. If you count more stitches than those listed in the gauge, use a larger hook to try and match the gauge. If you count fewer stitches, use a smaller hook. **This is important**: Work a new gauge swatch in the adjusted hook size to make sure you get the correct gauge before you start your project. You may need to try several hook sizes to make gauge. If you've done this and still can't match the suggested gauge, the yarn may be your culprit. Try a thicker yarn if your swatch has too many stitches per inch (cm); or thinner yarn if you have too few stitches.

Although some people dread making gauge swatches, they are a relatively small and easy way to check your tension before you get too far into a project. The gauge swatch is also a vehicle for practicing new stitches—make your mistakes in the swatch so that you can avoid them in the project.

TIP Making a gauge swatch will help you find the hook size that works for you, which means that you can crochet at your natural tension instead of worrying about how tightly or loosely to hold the hook. You'll actually save yourself time by checking your gauge—if your first swatch doesn't match the listed gauge, you'll only need to rip back a small square, instead of half of a sweater.

Skill Levels

Each pattern lists a skill level—a guide to the difficulty of the stitches and techniques used in the pattern. To help you decide whether you will attempt a pattern, read through the instructions to be sure you understand the general construction of the piece and determine whether any unfamiliar stitches are used in the design. Practice new-to-you stitches with stash yarn, and you'll have the confidence to get going with the project. Complete instructions for basic and advanced stitches can be found in the Appendix, page 146.

Here's how the skill levels are defined in this book.

Easy: Pattern uses basic stitches, repetitive stitch patterns, simple color changes, working in the round, simple shaping, and finishing. Beginners should be able to complete these with some focus.

Intermediate: Pattern uses a variety of techniques such as basic lace patterns or color patterns, more complex work in the round, and mid-level shaping and finishing. A few patterns will include machine sewing.

Experienced: Pattern uses intricate or non-repeating stitch patterns and techniques, colorwork, and detailed shaping and finishing.

Stitch Abbreviations

Reading crochet patterns can take some getting used to, but be patient with yourself and remember that with practice, you will learn all of the abbreviations. The patterns in this book use standard crochet abbreviations as listed in the chart at right—refer to this list if you're unsure of what each abbreviation stands for. For detailed instructions on making each stitch, turn to the Appendix (page 146). If you are in a country outside of the United States, you may know your stitches by different names. Please refer to the conversion chart at right before beginning any pattern to ensure that you are working the same stitch as I worked in the pattern.

STANDARD CROCHET ABBREVIATIONS

BP	back post
BL	work in the back loop(s) of the stitch
ch	chain
ch-lp/ch-sp	refers to a series of chains previously made, usually identified with a number, for example, ch-2 lp means "chain-2 loop," ch-2 sp means "chain-2 space"
dc	double crochet
dc2tog	double crochet 2 stitches together
esc	extended single crochet
fdc	foundation double crochet
FP	front post
hdc	half double crochet
hdc2tog	half double crochet 2 stitches together
lp(s)	loop(s)
RS	right side of work
sc	single crochet
sc2tog	single crochet 2 stitches together
sk	skip
sl st	slip stitch
sp(s)	space(s)
st(s)	stitch(es)
tog	together
tr	treble crochet
WS	wrong side of work
yo	yarn over (wrap yarn over hook)
*	Repeat the directions following the asterisk as many times as indicated.
**	Repeat the directions between the asterisks as many times as directed.
( )	Work directions inside parenthesis into the stitch indicated.
[ ]	Work the directions inside the bracket as many times as indicated.

CONVERSION CHART

US TERM	UK/AUS TERM
sl st slip stitch	**sc** single crochet
sc single crochet	**dc** double crochet
hdc half double crochet	**htr** half treble crochet
dc double crochet	**tr** treble crochet
tr treble crochet	**dtr** double treble crochet

Symbol Diagrams

Motifs and stitch patterns can be difficult to visualize, so whenever possible, I've included crochet symbol diagrams for visual reference. You can refer to both the symbol diagram and the written instructions for help working the patterns in this book. The Master Stitch Key below lists the diagram symbols for basic and commonly used crochet stitches. To further help you identify the symbols, a project-specific stitch key is included with each pattern.

Rows of stitches on symbol charts are read as follows:
Right-side rows: Right to left
Wrong-side rows: Left to right

The diagram is a visual representation of the work as it appears from the right side, to a right-handed crocheter. Therefore, you read the wrong-side rows "backward" because you will have turned the work before stitching that row. If you are left-handed, you will still read right-side rows from right to left, but you will work them from left to right, due to your hand's orientation. The same goes for wrong-side rows: If you are left-handed, read these rows from left to right, and work them from right to left.

Diagrams of stitch patterns worked in the round are read counterclockwise (just the same way you work the stitches, if you are right-handed) for right-side rounds. If you are left-handed, read the stitches on the chart in a counterclockwise direction, but work them in a clockwise manner.

Begin reading diagrams worked in the round at the center—there will be a symbol for an adjustable ring or a chain ring to begin. Each round of the diagram will be labeled with a number that corresponds to the same round in the written instructions. In the sample diagram below for the flower in the Cozy Crawlers Leg Warmers (page 68), Round 1 starts with a chain stitch (⌒) just to the left of the round number, then shows 10 single crochet stitches (+) worked in the ring. Round 1 ends with the black slip stitch (•) just above the first chain, which is used to join the round.

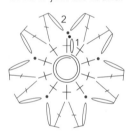

FLOWER

MASTER STITCH KEY

◎	= adjustable ring		⌇	= Front Post double crochet (FPdc)
⌒	= chain (ch)		⌇	= Back Post double crochet (BPdc)
•	= slip st (sl st)		⑁	= foundation double crochet (Fdc)
+	= single crochet (sc)		⸙	= extended single crochet (esc)
T	= half double crochet (hdc)		⟨⟩	= cluster (Cl)
⟊	= double crochet (dc)		⋀	= dc2tog
⟊	= treble crochet		⋀	= hdc2tog
—	= worked in back loop only		⋏	= sc2tog
▬	= worked in front loop only			

To make the diagrams easy to read, alternate rows and rounds are shown in contrasting colors, and Round 2 begins with the chain (⌒) just to the left of the round number. Then a "petal" consisting of 2 double crochet stitches (┤) is worked into the next sc (+), another chain stitch is worked (⌒), and then a slip stitch (•) is worked into the next single crochet (+) of the first round.

To continue working the round, read the diagram in a counterclockwise direction, and you'll see that you are simply repeating the petal sequence described above. For complete instruction on working crochet in the round, refer to the Appendix, page 146.

Remember: You can always use the written instructions to help you read the diagrams. You might also choose to avoid them altogether, if you're more comfortable with traditional patterns—complete instructions are included in the written pattern.

Schematics

The schematic is another important visual for clothing patterns. This drawing labels the measurements of each pattern piece and outlines their basic shapes. Arrows on the schematic indicate the direction in which you will crochet the pieces. If there is no arrow on the schematic, the piece will be crocheted from the bottom edge upward. As you are working, it's a good idea to measure your work and compare it to the schematic to be sure you are achieving the desired measurements. It's possible for your gauge to change as you become more familiar with the pattern, so check frequently to make sure that you maintain a consistent tension. If that doesn't seem to be the problem, you may have made a mistake somewhere along the way—try asking an expert for help at your local yarn shop.

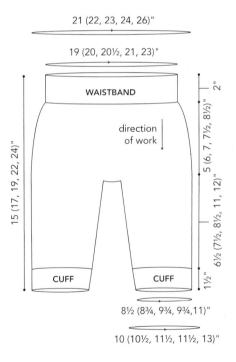

2

LITTLe
nursery

MIX AND MATCH MOTIF BLANKET

This vibrant blanket is the perfect gift for babies whose parents love color. Although it might look complicated at first glance, each square is made by applying simple color changes and embroidery to the same basic square pattern. You're sure to find at least a few colors to start with in your stash, and you can easily make a bigger blanket if you have more yarn (and time) on your hands!

SKILL LEVEL
Intermediate

SIZE	one size
FINISHED BLANKET	27½" (70cm) square
COLOR A	279 yd (256m)
COLORS B AND C	186 yd (171m) each
COLORS D, E, F, AND G	93 yd (85m) each

MATERIALS
1,023 yards (939m) of worsted-weight yarn: 11 skeins of Nashua Handknits *Julia*, 50% wool, 25% alpaca, 25% mohair, 93 yards (85m) 1¾ oz (50g); 3 skeins of #6396 Deep Blue Sea (A), 2 skeins each of #4726 Maine Coast Blue (B) and #5185 Spring Green (C), and 1 skein each of #0178 Harvest Spice (D), #0120 Squash (E), #1715 Rose (F), and #1784 Gourd (G) (4)

Size I-9 (5.5mm) crochet hook, *or size to obtain gauge*

Yarn needle

GAUGE
One completed motif measures 5¼" (13cm) square.

INSTRUCTIONS

Basic Motif

NOTE: *Each motif style is based on the basic motif pattern. Use the charts that follow to adapt the basic pattern as indicated.*

Ch 4; join with sl st in first ch to form a ring.

Round 1 (RS) Ch 3 (counts as dc here and throughout), 15 dc in ring; join with sl st in top of beginning ch—16 dc.

Round 2 Ch 3, dc in same st as join, 2 dc in each dc around; join with sl st in top of beginning ch—32 dc.

Round 3 Ch 3, 2 dc in next dc, [dc in next dc, 2 dc in next dc] 15 times; join with sl st in top of beginning ch—48 dc. Fasten off first color.

Round 4 (Ch 3, 2 dc, ch 2, 3 dc) in same st as join (corner made), [sk next 2 dc, sc in next 7 dc, sk next 2 dc, (3 dc, ch 2, 3 dc) in next dc (corner made)] 3 times, sk next 2 dc, sc in next 7 dc, sk next 2 dc; join with sl st in top of beginning ch—28 sc, 24 dc, and 4 corner ch-2 sps.

Round 5 Ch 2 (counts as hdc here and throughout), hdc in next 2 sts, [(2 hdc, ch 2, 2 hdc) in next corner ch-2 sp, hdc in next 13 sts] 3 times, (2 hdc, ch 2, 2 hdc) in next corner ch-2 sp, hdc in last 10 sts; join with sl st in beginning ch—68 hdc and 4 corner ch-2 sps.

Fasten off.

SOLID CIRCLE MOTIF (make 5 as instructed)

Work one of each motif as for the basic motif, changing colors for each round as indicated below.

MOTIF NAME	ROUNDS 1–3	ROUNDS 4 & 5
Solid Circle Motif 1	F	A
Solid Circle Motif 2	A	D
Solid Circle Motif 3	E	C
Solid Circle Motif 4	E	D
Solid Circle Motif 5	D	B

EMBROIDERED CIRCLE MOTIF

(make 5 as instructed)

Work one of each motif as for the basic motif, changing colors for each round as indicated below. Once each motif is complete, thread a yarn needle with a 36" (91.5cm) length of yarn. Thread the yarn in and out of top of the dc stitches of Round 1, fasten off and weave in all ends. Repeat this process with 2 more colors, threading one color per round through the dc stitches of Rounds 2 and 3, respectively.

MOTIF NAME	ROUNDS 1–3	ROUNDS 4 & 5	EMBROIDERY COLORS (Rounds 1, 2, 3)
Embroidered Circle Motif 1	C	B	B, G, D
Embroidered Circle Motif 2	C	G	D, E, F
Embroidered Circle Motif 3	G	E	C, A, B
Embroidered Circle Motif 4	F	C	C, B, A
Embroidered Circle Motif 5	B	F	F, D, C

CONCENTRIC CIRCLES MOTIF

(make 5 as instructed)

Work one of each motif as for the basic motif, changing colors for each round as indicated below.

MOTIF NAME	ROUND 1	ROUND 2	ROUND 3	ROUNDS 4 & 5
Concentric Circles Motif 1	A	F	A	B
Concentric Circles Motif 2	G	D	G	A
Concentric Circles Motif 3	D	C	D	F
Concentric Circles Motif 4	C	E	C	D
Concentric Circles Motif 5	E	A	E	G

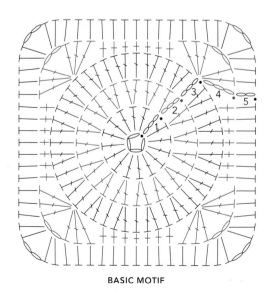

BASIC MOTIF

STITCH KEY

◠ = chain (ch)

• = slip st (sl st)

+ = single crochet (sc)

⊤ = half double crochet (hdc)

⧸ = double crochet (dc)

TARGET MOTIF (make 5 as instructed)

Work one of each motif as for the Basic Circle Motif, changing colors for each round as indicated below.

MOTIF NAME	ROUND 1	ROUND 2	ROUND 3	ROUNDS 4 & 5
Target Motif 1	D	B	E	G
Target Motif 2	E	C	F	D
Target Motif 3	F	D	B	A
Target Motif 4	B	F	D	A
Target Motif 5	B	G	C	A

PINWHEEL MOTIF (make 5 as instructed)

Work one of each motif, alternating colors as directed for Rounds 1–3. Crochet over the color not in use as you go, bringing it up to change colors on the last yarn over of the last stitch before the color change. Remember, you'll also need to change colors at the last yarn over of the round (before joining).

With first color, ch 4; join with sl st in first ch to form a ring.

Round 1 (RS) Ch 3 (counts as dc here and throughout), dc in ring [change to 2nd color, 2 dc in ring, change to first color, 2 dc in ring] 3 times, change to 2nd color, 2 dc in ring; join with sl st in top of beginning ch—16 dc.

Round 2 With first color, ch 3, dc in first st, 2 dc in next dc, [change to 2nd color, 2 dc in next 2 dc, change to first color, 2 dc in next 2 dc] 3 times, change to 2nd color, 2 dc in next 2 dc; join with sl st in top of beginning ch—32 dc.

Round 3 With first color, ch 3, 2 dc in next dc, dc in next dc, 2 dc in next dc, *change to 2nd color, [dc in next dc, 2 dc in next dc] twice, change to first color, [dc in next dc, 2 dc in next dc] twice; repeat from * 2 more times, change to 2nd color, [dc in next dc, 2 dc in next dc] twice; join with sl st in top of beginning ch—48 dc. Fasten off both colors.

Rounds 4 and 5 Using 3rd color, work Rounds 4 and 5 of basic motif.

MOTIF NAME	ROUNDS 1–3 (1st color)	ROUNDS 1–3 (2nd color)	ROUNDS 4 & 5 (3rd color)
Pinwheel Motif 1	A	F	C
Pinwheel Motif 2	G	C	A
Pinwheel Motif 3	A	C	G
Pinwheel Motif 4	B	D	E
Pinwheel Motif 5	E	F	D

This blanket makes a great gift for a virtual baby shower. Friends and family can send a few squares each to a designated person who can seam, edge, and deliver the blanket. Think of it as the crocheted version of a friendship quilt.

Finishing

Arrange the motifs following the assembly diagram below and sew the squares together as desired (Finishing Techniques, page 152).

Solid Circle Motif 1	Target Motif 1	Pinwheel Motif 1	Solid Circle Motif 2	Embroidered Circle Motif 1
Target Motif 2	Embroidered Circle Motif 3	Concentric Circles Motif 1	Embroidered Circle Motif 2	Concentric Circles Motif 2
Concentric Circles Motif 5	Pinwheel Motif 2	Solid Circle Motif 4	Concentric Circles Motif 3	Solid Circle Motif 3
Embroidered Circle Motif 4	Concentric Circles Motif 4	Target Motif 4	Pinwheel Motif 3	Target Motif 3
Pinwheel Motif 4	Solid Circle Motif 5	Embroidered Circle Motif 5	Target Motif 5	Pinwheel Motif 5

BORDER

Round 1 (RS) Join A with a sl st in any corner ch-2 sp, (ch 3, dc, ch 2, 2 dc) in same ch-sp, *[dc in each hdc to corner ch-sp of current square, dc in ch-sp, dc in corner ch-sp of next square] 4 times, dc in each hdc to next corner of blanket, (2 dc, ch 2, 2 dc) in corner ch-sp; repeat from * 2 more times, [dc in each hdc to corner ch-sp of current square, dc in ch-sp, dc in corner ch-sp of next square] 4 times, dc in each hdc to first corner of blanket; join with sl st in top of beginning ch—388 dc and 4 ch-2 sps.

Round 2 (RS) Ch 3, dc in next dc, (2 dc, ch 2, 2 dc) in corner ch-2 sp, dc in each dc around, working (2 dc, ch 2, 2 dc) in remaining corner ch-2 sps; join with sl st in top of beginning ch—404 dc and 4 ch-2 sps.

Round 3 (RS) With B, ch 1, sc in each dc around, working 4 sc in each corner ch-2 sp; join with sl st in first sc— 408 sc.

Fasten off.

Thread a yarn needle with a 48" (122cm) length of C. Weave the yarn in and out of the top of the dc stitches of Round 1 of the border along one edge of the blanket. Repeat for remaining 3 edges.

Weave in all ends.

TEXTURED BLANKET

This easy-to-memorize pattern of shells and post stitches
makes it a relaxing project for crocheters who are expecting.
The raised stitches create a texture that babies will love to
touch, and since it's worked in a worsted-weight yarn, you can
easily substitute the fiber of your choice to make a gift that
fits your budget.

SKILL LEVEL
Intermediate

SIZE	one size
FINISHED MEASUREMENTS	37" (94cm) wide x 40" (101.5cm) long
YARN NEEDED	1,220 yards (1,116m)

MATERIALS
1,220 yards (1,116m) of worsted-weight yarn: 13 skeins of Debbie Bliss *Cashmerino Aran*, 55% merino wool, 33% microfiber, 12% cashmere, 98 yards (80m), 1¾ oz (50g), color #202 light blue (4)

Size 7 (4.5mm) crochet hook, *or size to obtain gauge*

Yarn needle

GAUGE
18 sts and 10 rows = 4" (10cm) over pattern.

SPECIAL STITCHES
Front Post Double Crochet (FPdc) and Back Post Double Crochet (BPdc): Advanced Stitches, page 152.

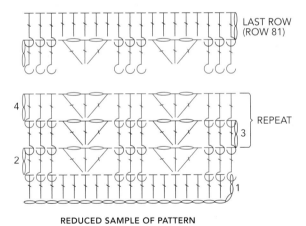

REDUCED SAMPLE OF PATTERN

STITCH KEY
- = chain (ch)
- = double crochet (dc)
- = Front Post double crochet (FPdc)
- = Back Post double crochet (BPdc)

INSTRUCTIONS
Ch 149.

Row 1 (RS) Dc in 4th ch from hook (beginning ch counts as first dc) and in each ch across—147 dc.

Row 2 Ch 2 (does not count as a st here and throughout), turn, *BPdc in next 3 sts, sk next 2 sts, (dc, ch 1, dc, ch 1, dc) in next st (shell made), sk next 2 sts; repeat from * across to last 3 sts, BPdc in last 3 sts—57 BPdc and 18 shells.

Row 3 Ch 2, turn, *FPdc in next 3 BPdc, sk next dc and ch-1 sp, (dc, ch 1, dc, ch 1, dc) in next dc (shell made), sk next ch-1 sp and dc; repeat from * across to last 3 sts, FPdc in last 3 BPdc—57 FPdc and 18 shells.

Row 4 Ch 2, turn, *BPdc in next 3 FPdc, sk next dc and ch-1 sp, (dc, ch 1, dc, ch 1, dc) in next st (shell made), sk next ch-1 sp and dc; repeat from * across to last 3 sts, BPdc in last 3 FPdc.

Rows 5–80 Repeat last 2 rows 38 times.

Row 81 Ch 2, turn, *FPdc in next 3 BPdc, dc in next 5 sts; repeat from * across to last 3 sts, FPdc in last 3 BPdc—57 FPdc and 90 dc.

Fasten off.

FINISHING
Weave in all ends.

TRY THIS!

Substitute Debbie Bliss *Cashmerino Aran* in # 36 Violet.

sweet dreams sleep sack

This snuggly sleeping bag is worked with a simple variation on the single crochet stitch that creates a fluffy, stretchy fabric to keep your child cozy in his or her crib. The front zipper makes it easy to get your baby ready for bed. Use the sack as an outer layer over pajamas, and it won't need daily laundering.

SKILL LEVEL
Experienced

SIZES	0–6 months	6–12 months	12–18 months	18–24 months
FINISHED CHEST	20½" (52cm)	22½" (57cm)	24½" (62cm)	26½" (67.5cm)
FINISHED LENGTH (to back neck)	21" (53.5cm)	22" (56cm)	23" (58.5cm)	24" (61cm)
COLOR A	540 yd (494m)	600 yd (549m)	670 yd (613m)	745 yd (681m)
COLOR B	160 yd (146m)	180 yd (165m)	205 yd (187m)	225 yd (206m)

MATERIALS
700 (780, 875, 970) yards (640 [713, 800, 887]m) of light worsted or DK-weight yarn: 3 (3, 4, 4) skeins Fiesta Yarns *Boomerang*, 100% superwash merino, 320 yards (294m), 5 oz (142g), 2 (2, 3, 3) skeins in #3931 Cochiti Lake Blue (A) and 1 skein #39138 Cool Breeze (B) (3)

Size I-9 (5.5mm) crochet hook, *or size to obtain gauge*

Size F-5 (3.75mm) crochet hook

Yarn needle

One zipper to match yarn, 22" (55cm) long

One snap closure, ⅝" (16mm) diameter

Sewing needle and thread

GAUGE
17 sts and 16 rows = 4" (10cm) over pattern stitch using the larger hook.

PATTERN STITCH
Worked over a multiple of 2 sts.

Row 1 Ch 1, turn, *sc in front loop of next st, sc in back loop of next st; repeat from * across.

Repeat Row 1 for pattern stitch.

REVERSE PATTERN STITCH
Worked over a multiple of 2 sts.

Row 1 Ch 1, turn, *sc in back loop of next st, sc in front loop of next st; repeat from * across.

Repeat Row 1 for pattern stitch.

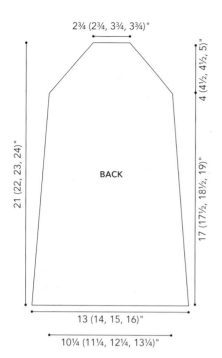

2¾ (2¾, 3¾, 3¾)"

4 (4½, 4½, 5)"

21 (22, 23, 24)"

BACK

17 (17½, 18½, 19)"

13 (14, 15, 16)"

10¼ (11¼, 12¼, 13¼)"

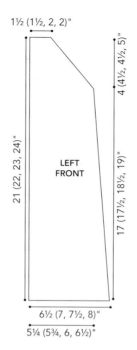

1½ (1½, 2, 2)"

4 (4½, 4½, 5)"

21 (22, 23, 24)"

LEFT FRONT

17 (17½, 18½, 19)"

6½ (7, 7½, 8)"

5¼ (5¾, 6, 6½)"

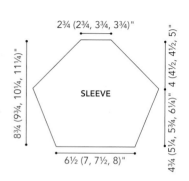

2¾ (2¾, 3¾, 3¾)"

4 (4½, 4½, 5)"

8¾ (9¾, 10¼, 11¼)"

SLEEVE

4¾ (5¼, 5¾, 6¼)"

6½ (7, 7½, 8)"

INSTRUCTIONS

Back

With larger hook and A, ch 57 (61, 65, 69).

Row 1 (WS) Sc in 2nd ch from hook and each ch across—56 (60, 64, 68) sc.

Rows 2–9 (11, 15, 17) Work Row 1 of pattern st 8 (10, 14, 16) times.

BEGIN SIDE SHAPING

Row 1 (RS) Ch 1, turn, sc2tog in back loop only over first 2 sts, *sc in front loop of next st, sc in back loop of next st; repeat from * across to last 2 sts, sc2tog in front loop only over last 2 sts—54 (58, 62, 66) sc.

Rows 2–10 Work Row 1 of reverse pattern st 9 times.

Row 11 (WS) Ch 1, turn, sc2tog in front loop only over first 2 sts, *sc in back loop of next st, sc in front loop of next st; repeat from * across to last 2 sts, sc2tog in back loop only over last 2 sts—52 (56, 60, 64) sc.

Rows 12–20 Work Row 1 of pattern st 9 times.

Rows 21–60 Repeat Rows 1–20 twice—44 (48, 52, 56) sc.

BEGIN ARMHOLE SHAPING

Row 1 (RS) Repeat Row 1 of Side Shaping—42 (46, 50, 54) sc.

Row 2 Repeat Row 11 of Side Shaping—40 (44, 48, 52) sc.

Rows 3–16 (18, 18, 20) Repeat Rows 1 and 2, 7 (8, 8, 9) times—12 (12, 16, 16) sc.

Fasten off.

Right Front

With larger hook and A, ch 29 (31, 33, 35).

Row 1 (WS) Sc in 2nd ch from hook and each ch across—28 (30, 32, 34) sc.

Rows 2–9 (13, 15, 17) Work Row 1 of pattern st 8 (12, 14, 16) times.

BEGIN SIDE SHAPING

Row 1 (RS) Ch 1, turn, *sc in front loop of next st, sc in back loop of next st; repeat from * across to last 2 sts, sc2tog in front loop only over last 2 sts—27 (29, 31, 33) sc.

Row 2 Ch 1, turn, sc in back loop of next st, *sc in front loop of next st, sc in back loop of next st; repeat from * across.

Row 3 Ch 1, turn, sc in front loop of next st, *sc in back loop of next st, sc in front loop of next st; repeat from * across.

Rows 4–9 Repeat Rows 2 and 3 three times.

Row 10 Repeat Row 2.

Row 11 (RS) Ch 1, turn, sc in front loop of next st, *sc in back loop of next st, sc in front loop of next st; repeat from * across to last 2 sts, sc2tog in back loop only over last 2 sts—26 (28, 30, 32) sc.

Rows 12–20 Work Row 1 of pattern st 9 times.

Rows 21–60 Repeat Rows 1–20 twice—22 (24, 26, 28) sc.

BEGIN ARMHOLE SHAPING

Row 1 (RS) Ch 1, turn, *sc in front loop of next st, sc in back loop of next st; repeat from * to last 2 sts, sc2tog over front loops only of last 2 sts—21 (23, 25, 27) sc.

Row 2 Ch 1, turn, sc2tog over front loops of next 2 sts, *sc in back loop of next st, sc in front loop of next st; repeat from * across to last st, sc in back loop of last st—20 (22, 24, 26) sc.

Rows 3–16 (18, 18, 20) Repeat Rows 1 and 2, 7 (8, 8, 9) times—6 (6, 8, 8) sc.

Fasten off.

Left Front

Work as for Right Front to Side Shaping.

BEGIN SIDE SHAPING

Row 1 (RS) Ch 1, turn, sc2tog in back loop over first 2 sts, *sc in front loop of next st, sc in back loop of next st; repeat from * across—27 (29, 31, 33) sc.

Row 2 Ch 1, turn, sc in front loop of next st, *sc in back loop of next st, sc in front loop of next st; repeat from * across.

Row 3 Ch 1, turn, sc in back loop of next st, *sc in front loop of next, sc in back loop of next st; repeat from * across.

Rows 4–9 Repeat Rows 2 and 3.

Row 10 Repeat Row 2.

Row 11 (RS) Ch 1, turn, sc2tog in front loop only over next 2 sts, *sc in back loop of next st, sc in front loop of next st; repeat from * across to last st, sc in back loop only of last st—26 (28, 30, 32) sc.

Rows 12–20 Work even in pattern st.

Rows 21–60 Repeat Rows 1–20 twice—22 (24, 26, 28) sc.

BEGIN ARMHOLE SHAPING

Row 1 (RS) Ch 1, turn, sc2tog in back loop only over first 2 sts, *sc in front loop of next st, sc in back loop of next st; repeat from * across—21 (23, 25, 27) sc.

Row 2 Ch 1, turn, *sc in front loop of next st, sc in back loop of next st; repeat from * across to last 3 sts, sc in front loop of next st, sc2tog in back loop only over last 2 sts—20 (22, 24, 26) sc.

Rows 3–16 (18, 18, 20) Repeat Rows 1 and 2, 7 (8, 8, 9) times—6, (6, 8, 8) sc.

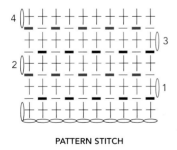

PATTERN STITCH

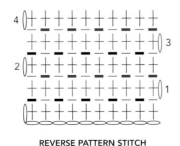

REVERSE PATTERN STITCH

STITCH KEY

⬯ = chain (ch)

+ = single crochet (sc)

— = worked in back loop only

▬ = worked in front loop only

Sizes 0–6 months (12–18 months) only

Rows 8–19 (23) Repeat Rows 4–7, 3 (4) times—44 (52) sc.

BEGIN CAP SHAPING (all sizes)

Row 1 (WS) Ch 1, turn, sc2tog in back loop only over first 2 sts, *sc in front loop of next st, sc in back loop of next st; repeat from * across to last 2 sts, sc2tog in front loop only over last 2 sts—42 (50) sc.

Row 2 (RS) Ch 1, turn, sc2tog in front loop only over first 2 sts, *sc in back loop of next st, sc in front loop of next st; repeat from * across to last 2 sts, sc2tog in back loop only over last 2 sts—40 (48) sc.

Rows 3–16 (18) Repeat Rows 1 and 2, 7 (8) times—12 (16) sc.

Fasten off.

Sizes 6–12 months (18–24 months) only

Rows 8–21 (25) Repeat Rows 4–7, 3 (4) times, then repeat Rows 4 and 5 once—48 (56) sc.

BEGIN CAP SHAPING (all sizes)

Row 1 (WS) Ch 1, turn, sc2tog in front loop only over first 2 sts, *sc in back loop of next st, sc in front loop of next st; repeat from * across to last 2 sts, sc2tog in back loop only over last 2 sts—46 (54) sc.

Row 2 (RS) Ch 1, turn, sc2tog in back loop only over first 2 sts, *sc in front loop of next st, sc in back loop of next st; repeat from * across to last 2 sts, sc2tog in front loop only over last 2 sts—44 (52) sc.

Rows 3–18 (20) Repeat Rows 1 and 2, 8 (9) times—12 (16) sc.

Fasten off.

Closure Tab

With larger hook and A, ch 10.

Round 1 Work 5 hdc in 3rd ch from hook, hdc in next 6 ch, 6 hdc in last ch; rotate to work across opposite side of foundation chain, hdc in next 6 ch; join with sl st in top of beginning ch—24 hdc.

Fasten off.

Sleeves (make 2)

With larger hook and B, ch 29 (31, 33, 35).

Row 1 Sc in 2nd ch from hook and each ch across—28 (30, 32, 34) sc.

Rows 2 and 3 Work Row 1 of pattern st twice.

Row 4 (RS) Ch 1, turn, sc in back loop of first st, sc in front loop of same st (increase made), *sc in back loop of next st, sc in front loop of next st; repeat from * across to last st, sc in back loop of last st, sc in front loop of same st (increase made)—30 (32, 34, 36) sc.

Row 5 Work Row 1 of reverse pattern st.

Row 6 (RS) Ch 1, turn, sc in front loop of first st, sc in back loop of same st (increase made), *sc in front loop of next st, sc in back loop of next st; repeat from * across to last st, sc in front loop of st, sc in back loop of same st (increase made)—32 (34, 36, 38) sc.

Row 7 Work Row 1 of pattern st.

Finishing

With right side facing and smaller hook, join A in the lower corner of one front piece, ch 1 and work sc evenly across front edge. Fasten off. Repeat to trim other front piece.

Working from the right sides of the pieces, slip stitch the sleeves to the back and fronts along the raglan sleeve edges, as follows: With the wrong sides together, and the sleeve on the bottom, align the armhole edge of the sleeve with the armhole edge of the back piece. Working through both thicknesses, join A with a slip stitch at the beginning of the armhole edge, slip stitch evenly across the edge to attach the sleeve to back. Fasten off. Repeat to attach the sleeve to the front. Then repeat to attach the other sleeve to the opposite armhole.

Fold the entire piece in half, with right sides together. Whipstitch the sleeve, side, and lower edges together (Whipstitch Seam, page 152). Turn the piece right side out.

With smaller hook and A, loosely slip stitch around the neck edge, and add 2 rows of single crochet around each sleeve.

Pin the zipper in place along the right front edge, starting at the neck, then hand sew the zipper in place. Repeat with the Left Front, unzipping the zipper as necessary to stitch it in place.

NOTE: *Depending on the size you are making, the zipper may be slightly shorter than the sleep sack. Working from the inside of the garment, whip stitch the edges of the garment below the zipper together with a length of yarn.*

Sew one curved end of the closure tab to the Right Front of the sleep sack just below the neckline. Sew a snap stud to the opposite end of the closure tab, and a snap socket to the Left Front of the sleep sack. Snap the tab in place to cover the zipper pull.

Weave in all ends.

TRY THIS!

Substitute Fiesta Yarns *Boomerang* in Disco Green (A) and Tutti Frutti (B).

sunshine blanket

Wrap your baby in rays of sunshine with this medium-weight lace blanket. Worked in a subtly toned sock yarn, the pretty petal design radiates from the center and continues to the outside edge of the blanket. If you love giving blankets but hate working foundation chains, this pattern is the one for you, as it's worked in the round from the very beginning. Be sure to start with a chain ring (instead of an adjustable ring), as it will stand up better to repeated washing.

SKILL LEVEL
Experienced

SIZE	one size
FINISHED MEASUREMENTS (in diameter)	43" (109cm) from point to point
YARN NEEDED	1140 yd (1042m)

MATERIALS
1140 yards (1042m) of sportweight yarn: 3 skeins of Blue Moon Fiber Arts *Socks that Rock Medium Weight*, 100% superwash merino, 380 yards (347m), 5½ oz (155g) in colorway Hoofle Floofle (**2**)

Size F-5 (3.75mm) crochet hook, *or size to obtain gauge*

Stitch markers (in 2 different colors, A and B)

Yarn needle

GAUGE
18 sts and 10 rows = 4" (10cm) over double crochet.

TIP If you make the blanket as written, you'll use up nearly every last inch of the recommended yarn—buy an extra ball to ensure you'll have enough. If you'd like to make a stroller-sized blanket that uses only 2 skeins of yarn, end the blanket after Round 34.

INSTRUCTIONS
NOTE: *Blanket is worked in joined rounds. Do not turn at the beginning of a round. The right side of the blanket is always facing you as you work.*

Ch 6; join with sl st in first ch to form a ring.

Round 1 (RS) Ch 3 (counts as first dc here and throughout), 15 dc in ring—16 dc.

Round 2 Ch 5 (counts as dc, ch 2 here and throughout), dc in same st as join, [sk next dc, (dc, ch 2, dc) in next dc] 7 times, sk last dc; join with sl st in 3rd ch of beginning ch—16 dc and 8 ch-2 sps.

Round 3 Sl st in first ch-2 sp, ch 3, 3 dc in first ch-2 sp, ch 1, [4 dc in next ch-2 sp, ch 1] 7 times; join with sl st in top of beginning ch—eight 4-dc groups and 8 ch-1 sps.

Round 4 Ch 3, 2 dc in next 2 dc, dc in next dc, ch 2, [sk next ch-1 sp, dc in next dc, 2 dc in next 2 dc, dc in next dc, ch 2] 7 times; join with sl st in top of beginning ch—eight 6-dc groups and 8 ch-2 sps.

Round 5 Ch 3, [dc2tog over next 2 dc] twice, dc in next dc, ch 2, dc in next ch-2 sp, ch 2, *dc in next dc, [dc2tog over next 2 dc] twice, dc in next dc, ch 2, dc in next ch-2 sp, ch 2; repeat from * around; join with sl st in top of beginning ch—40 dc and 16 ch-2 sps.

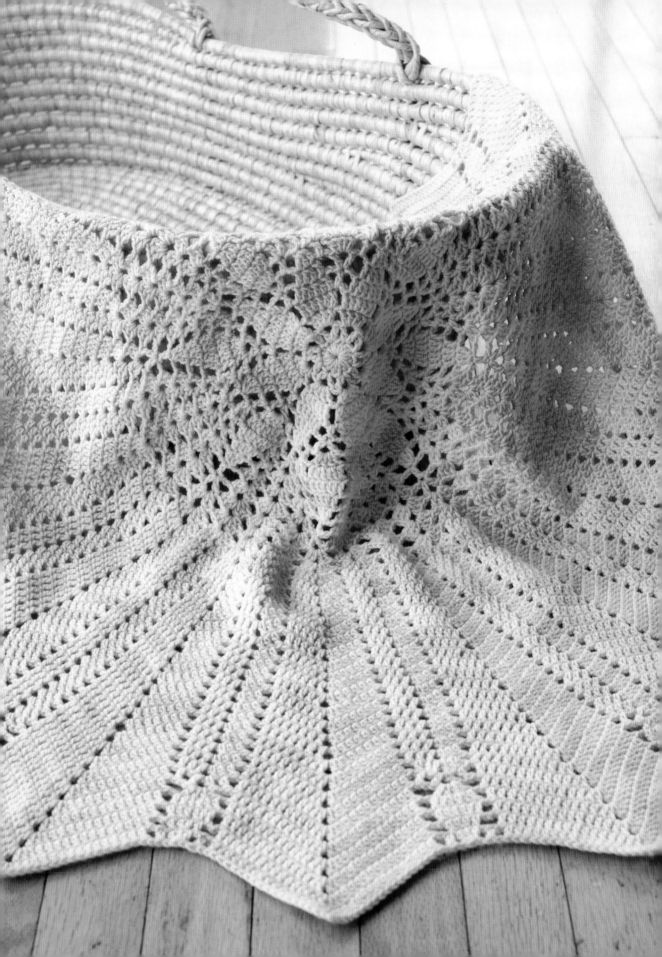

Round 6 Ch 3, dc2tog over next 2 dc, dc in next dc, ch 2, sk next ch-2 sp, (dc, ch 2, dc) in next dc, ch 2, sk next ch-2 sp, *dc in next dc, dc2tog over next 2 dc, dc in next dc, ch 2, sk next ch-2 sp, (dc, ch 2, dc) in next dc, ch 2, sk next ch-2 sp; repeat from * around; join with sl st in top of beginning ch—40 dc and 24 ch-2 sps.

Round 7 Ch 3, dc2tog over next 2 dc, ch 2, dc in next ch-2 sp, ch 2, 4 dc in next ch-2 sp, ch 2, dc in next ch-2 sp, ch 2, *dc3tog over next 3 dc, ch 2, dc in next ch-2 sp, ch 2, 4 dc in next ch-2 sp, ch 2, dc in next ch-2 sp, ch 2; repeat from * around; join with sl st in top of first dc2tog—56 dc and 32 ch-2 sps.

Round 8 Ch 5, sk first ch-2 sp, (dc, ch 2, dc) in next dc, ch 2, sk next ch-2 sp, dc in next dc, 2 dc in next 2 dc, dc in next dc, ch 2, sk next ch-2 sp, (dc, ch 2, dc) in next dc, ch 2, sk next ch-2 sp, *dc in next dc3tog, ch 2, sk next ch-2 sp, (dc, ch 2, dc) in next dc, ch 2, sk next ch-2 sp, dc in next dc, 2 dc in next 2 dc, dc in next dc, ch 2, sk next ch-2 sp, (dc, ch 2, dc) in next dc, ch 2, sk next ch-2 sp; repeat from * around; join with sl st in 3rd ch of beginning ch—72 dc and 48 ch-2 sps.

Round 9 Ch 5, dc in same st as join, sk next ch-2 sp, (dc, ch 2, dc) in next ch-2 sp, ch 2, sk next ch-2 sp, dc in next dc, [dc2tog over next 2 dc] twice, dc in next dc, ch 2, sk next ch-2 sp, (dc, ch 2, dc) in next ch-2 sp, sk next ch-2 sp, *(dc, ch 2, dc) in next ch-2 sp, sk next ch-2 sp, (dc, ch 2, dc) in next ch-2 sp, ch 2, sk next ch-2 sp, dc in next dc, [dc2tog over next 2 dc] twice, dc in next dc, ch 2, sk next ch-2 sp, (dc, ch 2, dc) in next ch-2 sp, sk next ch-2 sp; repeat from * around; join with sl st in 3rd ch of beginning ch—80 dc and 40 ch-2 sps.

Round 10 (Sl st, ch 3, dc, ch 2, 2 dc) in first ch-2 sp, (dc, ch 2, dc) in next ch-2 sp, ch 2, dc in next dc, dc2tog over next 2 dc, dc in next dc, ch 2, sk next ch-2 sp, (dc, ch 2, dc) in next ch-2 sp, *(2 dc, ch 2, 2 dc) in next ch-2 sp, (dc, ch 2, dc) in next ch-2 sp, ch 2, dc in next dc, dc2tog over next 2 dc, dc in next dc, ch 2, sk next ch-2 sp, (dc, ch 2, dc) in next ch-2 sp; repeat from * around; join with sl st in top of beginning ch—88 dc and 40 ch-2 sps.

Round 11 Sl st in next dc, (sl st, ch 3, dc, ch 2, 2 dc) in next ch-2 sp, (2 dc, ch 2, 2 dc) in next ch-2 sp, ch 2, sk next ch-2 sp, dc3tog over next 3 dc, ch 2, sk next ch-2 sp, *(2 dc, ch 2, 2 dc) in next 3 ch-2 sps, ch 2, sk next ch-2 sp, dc3tog over next 3 dc, ch 2, sk next ch-2 sp; repeat from * around to last ch-2 sp, (2 dc, ch 2, 2 dc) in last ch-2 sp; join with sl st in top of beginning ch—104 dc, and 40 ch-2 sps.

Round 12 Sl st in next dc, (sl st, ch 3, 2 dc, ch 2, 3 dc) in next ch-2 sp, (2 dc, ch 2, 2 dc) in next ch-2 sp, ch 2, sk next ch-2 sp, dc in next dc3tog, ch 2, sk next ch-2 sp, (2 dc, ch 2, 2 dc) in next ch-2 sp, *(3 dc, ch 2, 3 dc) in next ch-2 sp, (2 dc, ch 2, 2 dc) in next ch-2 sp, ch 2, sk next ch-2 sp, dc in next dc3tog, ch 2, sk next ch-2 sp, (2 dc, ch 2, 2 dc) in next ch-2 sp; repeat from * around; join with sl st in top of beginning ch—120 dc and 40 ch-2 sps.

Round 13 Sl st in next 2 dc, (sl st, ch 3, 2 dc, ch 2, 3 dc) in next ch-2 sp, (3 dc, ch 2, 3 dc) in next ch-2 sp, sk next ch-2 sp, (dc, ch 2, dc) in next dc, sk next ch-2 sp, *(3 dc, ch 2, 3 dc) in next 3 ch-2 sps, sk next ch-2 sp, (dc, ch 2, dc) in next dc, sk next ch-2 sp; repeat from * around to last ch-2 sp, (3 dc, ch 2, 3 dc) in last ch-2 sp; join with sl st in top of beginning ch—160 dc and 32 ch-2 sps.

Round 14 Sl st in next 2 dc, (sl st, ch 3, 2 dc, ch 2, 3 dc) in next ch-2 sp, (3 dc, ch 2, 3 dc) in next ch-2 sp, (2 dc, ch 2, 2 dc) in next ch-2 sp, *(3 dc, ch 2, 3 dc) in next 3 ch-2 sps, (2 dc, ch 2, 2 dc) in next ch-2 sp; repeat from * around to last ch-2 sp, (3 dc, ch 2, 3 dc) in last ch-2 sp; join with sl st in top of beginning ch—176 dc and 32 ch-2 sps.

Round 15 Sl st in next 2 dc, (sl st, ch 3, 2 dc, ch 2, 3 dc) in next ch-2 sp, (3 dc, ch 2, 3 dc) in each ch-2 sp around; join with sl st in top of beginning ch—192 dc and 32 ch-2 sps.

Round 16 Sl st in next dc, ch 3, dc in next dc, (dc, ch 2, dc) in next ch-2 sp, dc in next 2 dc, sk next 2 dc, dc in next 2 dc, (dc, ch 2, dc) in next ch-2 sp, dc in next 2 dc, sk next 2 dc, dc in next 2 dc, (2 dc, ch 2, 2 dc) in next ch-2 sp (shell made), dc in next 2 dc, sk next 2 dc, dc in next 2 dc, (dc, ch 2, dc) in next ch-2 sp, dc in next 2 dc, sk next 2 dc, *[dc in next 2 dc, (dc, ch 2, dc) in next ch-2 sp, dc in next 2 dc, sk next 2 dc] twice, dc in next 2 dc, (2 dc, ch 2, 2 dc) in next ch-2 sp (shell made), dc in next 2 dc, sk next 2 dc, dc in next 2 dc, (dc, ch 2, dc) in next ch-2 sp, dc in next 2 dc, sk next 2 dc; repeat from * around; join with sl st in top of beginning ch—208 dc and 32 ch-2 sps (consisting of shells arranged in 16 peaks and 16 valleys).

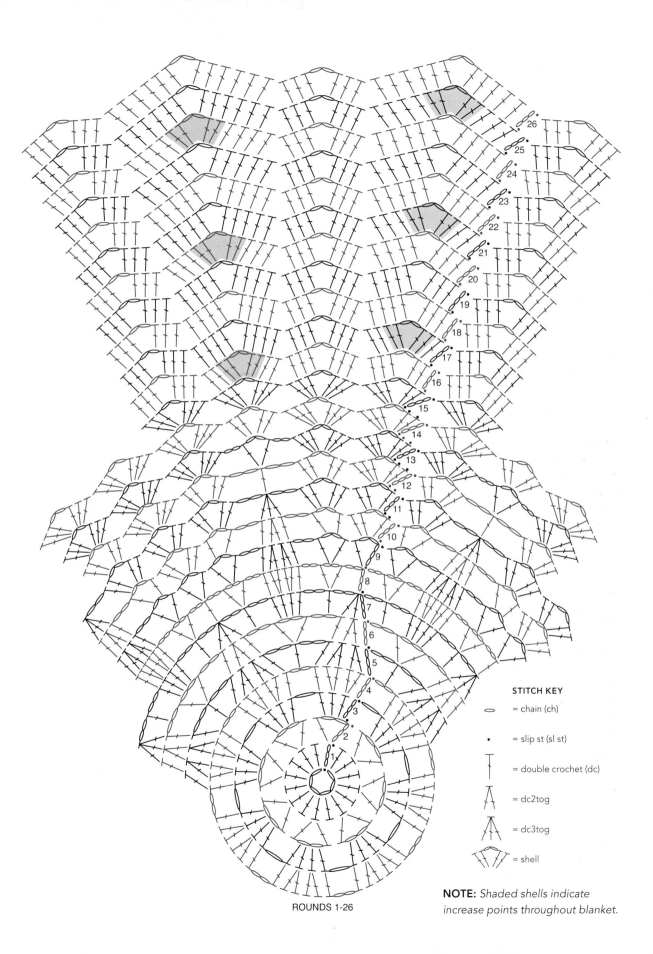

ROUNDS 1-26

STITCH KEY

⬯ = chain (ch)

• = slip st (sl st)

 = double crochet (dc)

 = dc2tog

 = dc3tog

 = shell

NOTE: *Shaded shells indicate increase points throughout blanket.*

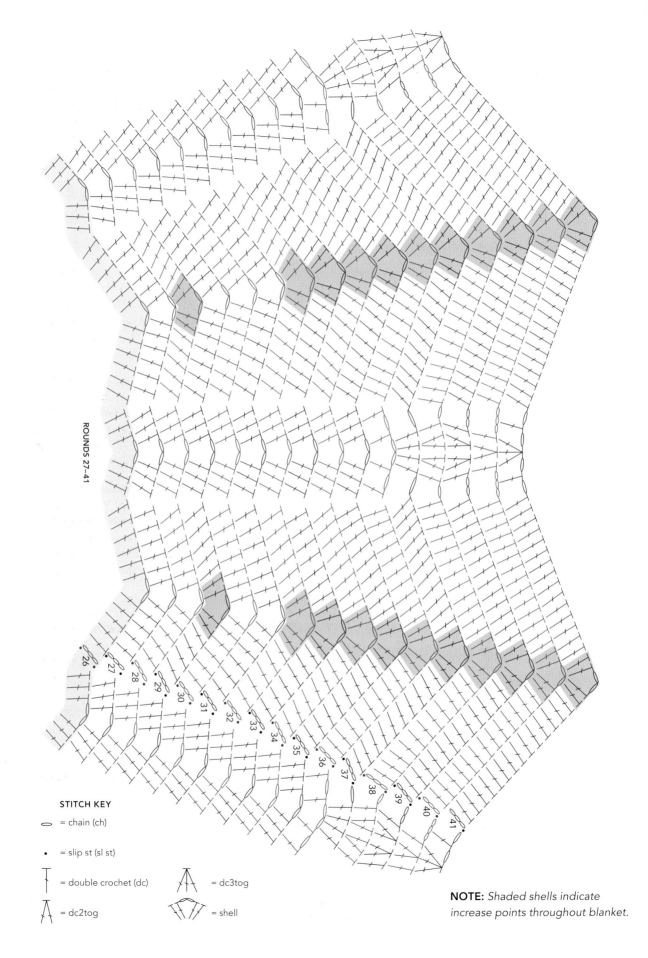

ROUNDS 27–41

STITCH KEY

⬯ = chain (ch)

• = slip st (sl st)

┬ = double crochet (dc)

⋀ = dc2tog

⋏ = dc3tog

⟨⟩ = shell

NOTE: *Shaded shells indicate increase points throughout blanket.*

Place color A stitch marker in center ch-2 sp of each (2 dc, ch 2, 2 dc) shell of Round 16. Move markers up as work progresses.

Round 17 Sl st in next dc, ch 3, dc in next dc, (2 dc, ch 2, 2 dc) in next ch-2 sp (shell made), dc in next 2 dc, sk next 2 dc, dc in next 2 dc, (dc, ch 2, dc) in next ch-2 sp, dc in next 2 dc, sk next 2 dc, dc in next 3 dc, (dc, ch 2, dc) in next ch-2 sp, dc in next 3 dc, sk next 2 dc, dc in next 2 dc, (dc, ch 2, dc) in next ch-2 sp, dc in next 2 dc, sk next 2 dc, *dc in next 2 dc, (2 dc, ch 2, 2 dc) in next ch-2 sp (shell made), dc in next 2 dc, sk next 2 dc, dc in next 2 dc, (dc, ch 2, dc) in next ch-2 sp, dc in next 2 dc, sk next 2 dc, dc in next 3 dc, (dc, ch 2, dc) in next ch-2 sp, dc in next 3 dc, sk next 2 dc, dc in next 2 dc, (dc, ch 2, dc) in next ch-2 sp, dc in next 2 dc, sk next 2 dc; repeat from * around; join with sl st in top of beginning ch—224 dc and 32 ch-2 sps.

Place color B stitch marker in center ch-2 sp of each (2 dc, ch 2, 2 dc) shell of Round 17.

Move markers up as work progresses.

Rounds 18 and 19 (work even) Sl st in next dc, ch 3, *dc in each dc to next ch-2 sp, (dc, ch 2, dc) in next ch-2 sp, dc in each dc to last dc of the dc-group (in the valley), sk next 2 dc (last dc of first dc-group, and first dc of next dc-group); repeat from * around; join with sl st in top of beginning ch.

Round 20 Sl st in next dc, ch 3, dc in each dc around, skipping the 2 dc in each valley, working (2 dc, ch 2, 2 dc) in each ch-2 sp marked with color A, and (dc, ch 2, dc) in all other ch-2 sps; join with sl st in top of beginning ch—240 dc and 32 ch-2 sps.

Round 21 Sl st in next dc, ch 3, dc in each dc around, skipping the 2 dc in each valley, working (2 dc, ch 2, 2 dc) in each ch-2 sp marked with color B, and (dc, ch 2, dc) in all other ch-2 sps; join with sl st in top of beginning ch—256 dc and 32 ch-2 sps.

Rounds 22 and 23 Repeat Round 18.

Rounds 24–31 Repeat Rounds 20–23 twice—320 dc and 32 ch-2 sps.

Rounds 32–35 Sl st in next dc, ch 3, dc in each dc around, skipping the 2 dc in each valley, working (2 dc, ch 2, 2 dc) in each ch-2 sp marked with color A or with color B, and (dc, ch 2, dc) in all unmarked ch-2 sps; join with sl st in top of beginning ch—448 dc and 32 ch-2 sps.

Round 36 Sl st in next dc, ch 3, *dc in each dc to next ch-2 sp, (2 dc, ch 2, 2 dc) in next ch-2 sp, dc in each dc to last dc of group, sk next 2 dc (in valley), dc in next dc, ch 1, (dc, ch 2, dc) in next ch-2 sp, ch 1, sk next dc, dc in next dc, sk next 2 dc; repeat from * around; join with sl st in top of beginning ch—448 dc and 32 ch-2 sps.

Round 37 Sl st in next dc, ch 3, *dc in each dc to next ch-2 sp, (2 dc, ch 2, 2 dc) in next ch-2 sp, dc in each dc to last dc of group, ch 1, sk next 3 dc, 4 dc in next ch-2 sp, ch 1, sk next 3 dc; repeat from * around; join with sl st in top of beginning ch—480 dc and 16 ch-2 sps.

Round 38 Sl st in next dc, ch 3, *dc in each dc to next ch-2 sp, (2 dc, ch 2, 2 dc) in next ch-2 sp, dc in each dc to last dc of group, ch 1, sk next dc, sk next ch-1 sp, dc in next dc, 2 dc in next 2 dc, dc in next dc, ch 1, sk next ch-1 sp, sk next dc; repeat from * around; join with sl st in top of beginning ch—544 dc and 16 ch-2 sps.

Round 39 Sl st in next dc, ch 3, *dc in each dc to next ch-2 sp, (2 dc, ch 2, 2 dc) in next ch-2 sp, dc in each dc to last dc of group, ch 2, sk next dc, sk next ch-1 sp, dc in next dc, [dc2tog over next 2 dc] twice, dc in next dc, ch 2, sk next ch-1 sp, sk next dc; repeat from * around; join with sl st in top of beginning ch—544 dc and 48 ch-2 sps.

Round 40 Sl st in next dc, ch 3, *dc in each dc to next ch-2 sp, (2 dc, ch 2, 2 dc) in next ch-2 sp, dc in each dc to last dc of group, ch 3, sk next dc, sk next ch-2 sp, dc in next dc, dc2tog over next 2 dc, dc in next dc, ch 3, sk next ch-2 sp, sk next dc; repeat from * around; join with sl st in top of beginning ch—560 dc, 16 ch-2 sps, and 32 ch-3 sps.

Round 41 Sl st in next dc, ch 3, *dc in each dc to next ch-2 sp, (2 dc, ch 2, 2 dc) in next ch-2 sp, dc in each dc to last dc of group, ch 1, dc in 2nd ch of next ch-3, ch 1, dc3tog over next 3 dc, ch 1, dc in 2nd ch of next ch-3, ch 1, sk next dc; repeat from * around; join with sl st in top of beginning ch—592 dc and 16 ch-2 sps.

Fasten off.

Finishing

Weave in all ends. To highlight the lace, block the blanket to the finished measurements.

birdie mobile

Make a flock of bright birdies for baby's crib to stimulate his interest in the world around him. Pick contrasting colors that are easy for young eyes to see and hang the mobile just out of your child's reach. You can also use this pattern to create simple stuffed toys or appliqués for your child's wardrobe.

SKILL LEVEL
Intermediate

SIZE	one size
FINISHED BIRD	4½" (11.5cm) long x 4¼" (11cm) tall
FINISHED MOBILE (assembled)	8" (20.5cm) in diameter x 16" (40.5cm) tall
YARN NEEDED	440 yd (402m)

MATERIALS

440 yards (402m) of worsted-weight yarn: 1 skein each of Classic Elite Yarns *Jil Eaton: Minnow Merino*, 100% extra fine merino, 136 yards (84m), 1¾ oz (50g), #4720 Aqua (A), #4781 Green Grass (B), #4758 Rouge (C), and #4750 Goldie (D) (4)

Size G-6 (4mm) crochet hook, *or size to obtain gauge*

Size H-8 (5mm) crochet hook (for finishing)

Yarn needle

Polyester stuffing or wool roving

Sewing needle and matching sewing thread

Metal hoop, 7" (18cm) diameter

Hook (for hanging) and monofilament line, if desired

GAUGE
Gauge is not critical for this project. To check gauge, compare your bird to the finished measurements.

INSTRUCTIONS

Birdie (make 8, 2 birds per color)

BODY
Make an adjustable ring.

Row 1 Ch 3 (counts as dc here and throughout), 7 dc in ring—8 dc.

Row 2 Ch 3, turn, dc in first dc, 2 dc in each dc across, 2 dc in top of turning ch—16 dc.

Row 3 Ch 3, turn, 2 dc in next dc, [dc in next dc, 2 dc in next dc] 7 times—24 dc.

NOTE: *In the next round, stitches are worked all the way around the outer edge of the piece.*

Round 4 Ch 3, turn, dc in next dc, 2 dc in next dc, [dc in next 2 dc, 2 dc in next dc] 6 times, 2 dc in last 3 dc; ch 1, do not turn, working across top of bird, 2 sc in end of each of next 6 rows, sk end of next row, work 6 dc in sp between ends of last 2 rows; join with sl st in first dc—40 dc, and 12 sc. Do not fasten off.

HEAD

Row 5 Ch 3, turn, dc in same st as join, 2 dc in each of next 2 dc, hdc in next dc, sc in next dc, sl st in next dc; leave remaining sts unworked—8 sts.

Fasten off.

WING (make 8, 2 wings per color)

Make an adjustable ring.

Row 1 (WS) Ch 3, 5 dc in ring—6 dc.

Round 2 Ch 3, turn, dc in first dc, 2 dc in next 5 dc; ch 1, do not turn, working across top of wing, 2 sc in end of each row; join with sl st in top of turning ch—12 dc and 8 sc.

Fasten off, leaving an 8" (20.5cm) tail.

Finishing

NOTE: *Because there is marginal difference between the right and wrong side of each body piece, either side can face outward when sewing birdies together.*

Before sewing the wings to the body pieces, take each pair of body pieces and determine the outside of each piece. Ensure that the head of each pair faces in the same direction. Weave in beginning tail of each wing. Using long ending tail, sew the top edge of each wing to the outside of a body piece, using the following color combinations.

Bird 1 Sew A colored wings to C colored bodies.

Bird 2 Sew C colored wings to D colored bodies.

Bird 3 Sew B colored wings to A colored bodies.

Bird 4 Sew D colored wings to B colored bodies.

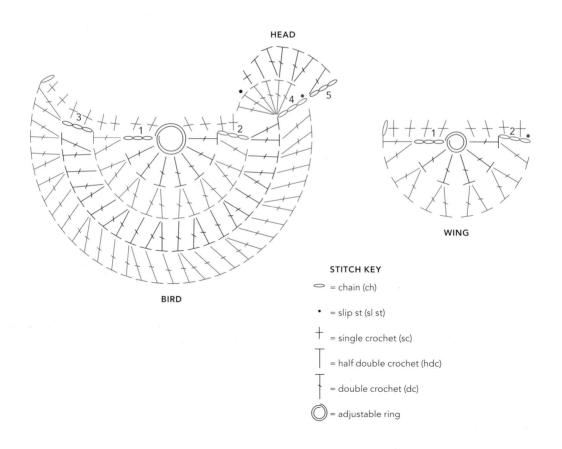

HEAD

BIRD

WING

STITCH KEY

⬯ = chain (ch)

• = slip st (sl st)

+ = single crochet (sc)

T = half double crochet (hdc)

🕇 = double crochet (dc)

◎ = adjustable ring

Your chain strands should cross and connect at the top of the mobile—at this point they will slide around a lot. Next, you'll wrap the ring in sl sts worked around the hoop in order to space out the chain strands you just made and assure that the birds will remain evenly spaced instead of sliding around the hoop.

To begin, with smaller hook and 1 strand of C, make a slipknot and place it on your hook. Hold the hoop in your lap vertically. Hold your hook just over the hoop, with yarn behind the ring. Yarn over and pull the loop through your slipknot, *move hook over top (outside) of ring, yarn over and pull the loop through the loop on your hook, bring hook to bottom (inside) of ring, yarn over and pull the loop through the loop on your hook*; repeat from * to * 49 times, **remove hook, bring working loop and yarn behind cross-chain attaching next bird, reinsert hook, repeat from * to * 50 times**; repeat from ** to ** twice more. Fasten off and weave in all ends.

Place a hook at the top of the mobile where the chain strands cross, and hang, or use monofilament line if desired.

BIRDIE ASSEMBLY

Place two birds together, with winged sides out. With same color as wing, join the yarn in the edge at center bottom of the bird, ch 1, working through both thicknesses, sc evenly around the outer edge, working 3 sc in the corner stitch of the tail and beak. Stop before you work all the way around, leaving a 3" (7.5cm) opening, and stuff the bird. Once the bird is stuffed, continue to sc around the outer edge, and join the last sc to the first with a sl st.

MOBILE CONSTRUCTION

With larger hook and 2 strands of A, use a sl st to join yarn to center sc along top edge of Bird 1. Ch 20, bring yarn behind metal hoop, ch 1 (encasing hoop), ch 31 (extending chain across to other side of hoop), ch 1 around hoop, ch 19, insert hook in center sc of Bird 2 and sl st, attaching Bird 2. Fasten off.

With larger hook and 2 strands of A held together, use a sl st to join yarn to center sc along top edge of Bird 3, ch 35, ch 1 (encasing hoop), ch 15, insert hook in 16th chain extending across top of hoop from Bird 1 to Bird 2, sl st, ch 15, ch 1 (encasing other side of hoop), ch 34, insert hook in top sc of Bird 4, and sl st to attach bird. Fasten off.

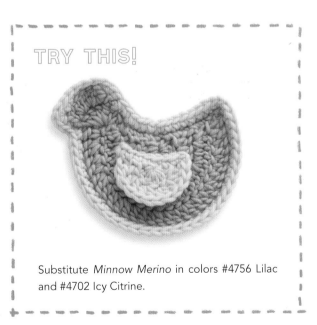

TRY THIS!

Substitute *Minnow Merino* in colors #4756 Lilac and #4702 Icy Citrine.

FELTED PLAY RUG

Bulky yarn and simple single crochet make this chunky rug a perfect first project for beginners who want to try their hand at changing colors and working in the round. Felt the rug by throwing it in the washing machine after you've finished stitching it; the felting process will shrink the fabric and conceal any minor mistakes in your work.

SKILL LEVEL
Easy

SIZE	one size
FINISHED MEASUREMENTS (diameter)	43" (109cm) before felting and 35" (89cm) after felting
COLORS A AND D	260 yd (239m) each
COLORS B AND C	130 yd (120m) each

MATERIALS

610 yds (560m) of 100% wool super bulky yarn: 6 skeins of Brown Sheep Company *Burly Spun*, 100% wool, 132 yards (121m), 8 oz (226g), 2 skeins each #110 Orange You Glad (A) and #79 Blue Boy (D), 1 skein each of # 78 Aztec Turquoise (B), and #120 Limeade (C) (6)

NOTE: *Make sure to use 100% wool for the best results. Do not use superwash wool, as it will not felt. Felt a swatch of your chosen yarn to make sure it is well suited for the project.*

Size N-15 (10mm) crochet hook, *or size to obtain gauge*

Stitch markers in two colors

Yarn needle

Top-loading washing machine, liquid dish soap, and old jeans (for felting)

GAUGE
First 5 rounds = 4½" (12cm) in diameter.

INSTRUCTIONS

NOTES: *Rug is worked in a continuous spiral; do not join rounds and do not turn at the end of rounds.*

To keep track of your work, mark the end of the round with a stitch marker and move it up at the end of each round.

With A, make an adjustable ring.

Round 1 (RS) Ch 1, 6 sc in ring—6 sc.

Round 2 Work 2 sc in each sc around—12 sc.

Round 3 [Sc in next sc, 2 sc in next sc (increase made)] 6 times—18 sc.

Round 4 [Sc in next 2 sc, 2 sc in next sc] 6 times—24 sc.

Round 5 [Sc in next 3 sc, 2 sc in next sc] 6 times—30 sc.

Round 6 [Sc in next 4 sc, 2 sc in next sc, place marker in last sc made] 6 times—36 sc.

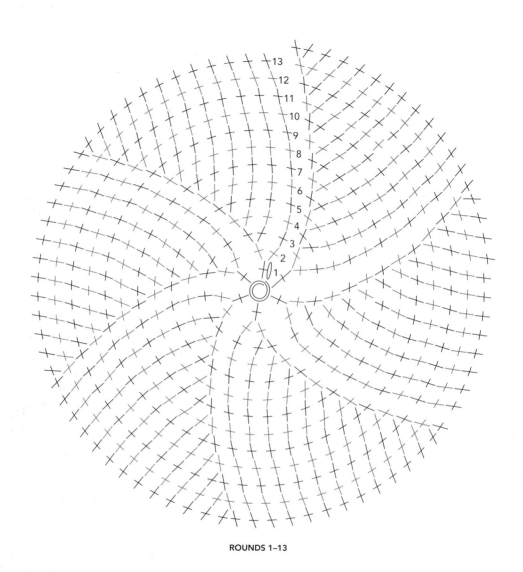

ROUNDS 1–13

STITCH KEY

 = chain (ch)

+ = single crochet (sc)

◎ = adjustable ring

FELTING

Set your washing machine to the hot wash cycle and add a teaspoon of liquid dish soap to the wash. Let the washer fill, place your rug and several old pairs of jeans in the washer, and allow the wash cycle to run. Check the rug near the end of the cycle, and if it is felted as desired, set machine to cool rinse and finish the cycle. If you'd like to felt the rug further, turn the dial back and let the hot wash repeat the cycle as many times as necessary. Roll the rug in a towel and gently squeeze out the excess water, then lay the rug flat to dry, straightening and pinning the edges neatly in place. The rug may take several days to dry completely.

NOTE: *To keep the rug from felting further, wash it by hand in cool water when necessary or spot clean.*

Continue working in rounds, working 2 single crochet stitches into the marked stitches of each round. Move the markers up to the 2nd single crochet of each 2 sc increase as you go. To avoid confusion, be sure to use markers that differ in color from the marker indicating the beginning of the round. Change yarn colors as directed below, remembering to change in the last yarn over in the last stitch of the round before the new color begins.

Rounds 7–12 Work with A.

Rounds 13–16 Work with B.

Rounds 17–18 Work with C.

Rounds 19–26 Work with D.

Round 27 Work with B.

Rounds 28–35 Work with A.

Round 36–38 Work with C.

Rounds 39–45 Work with B.

Fasten off. Weave in all ends.

TRY THIS!

Substitute Brown Sheep Company *Burly Spun* in colors #59 Periwinkle (A), #120 Limeade, #78 Aztec Turquoise and #62 Amethyst.

3

LITTLe
CLOTHes

Boat Neck sweater

This classic pullover works up quickly with minimal shaping and easy double crochet stitches, and two optional buttons at the shoulder provide plenty of headway for wiggly kids. Working the stripes in three colors makes it simple to switch strands after you complete each row, but if you're looking for something truly simple, work the entire sweater in a solid color.

SKILL LEVEL
Easy

SIZES	0–6 months	6–12 months	12–18 months	2 years	3 years
FINISHED CHEST	20" (51cm)	22" (56cm)	24" (61cm)	25" (63.5cm)	26" (66cm)
FINISHED LENGTH	11" (28cm)	12" (30.5cm)	13" (33cm)	14½" (37cm)	15½" (39.5cm)
COLOR A	155 yd (142m)	175 yd (160m)	200 yd (183m)	230 yd (210m)	240 yd (219m)
COLORS B AND C (each)	125 yd (114m)	140 yd (128m)	160 yd (146m)	185 yd (169m)	195 yd (178m)

MATERIALS
405 (455, 520, 600, 630) yards (370 [416, 475, 549, 572])m of sportweight yarn: 3 (4, 6, 6, 6) skeins Tahki Yarns *Cotton Classic Lite*, 100% mercerized cotton, 146 yards (135m), 1¾ oz (50g), 1 (2, 2, 2, 2) skein(s) color #4870 Dark Bright Blue (A) and 1 (1, 2, 2, 2) skein(s) each #4001 White (B) and #4402 Dark Orange (C) (**2**)

Size F-5 (3.75mm) crochet hook, *or size to obtain gauge*

Yarn needle

Two fish-shaped buttons, ⅝" (15mm) diameter (optional)

Sewing needle and thread

Stitch markers

GAUGE
18 sts = 4" (10cm) and 7 rows = 3" (7.5cm) over double crochet.

STRIPE PATTERN
*Work one row with A, one row with B, one row with C; repeat from * throughout.

INSTRUCTIONS
NOTE: *Change colors at the end of each row. For the best results, remember to change colors on the last yarn over of the last stitch of the row with the old color. Carry the unused colors up the side as the work progresses.*

Back
With A, ch 48 (52, 56, 58, 60).

Row 1 (RS) Dc in 4th ch from hook (beginning ch counts as dc) and in each ch across—46 (50, 54, 56, 58) dc.

Row 2 (WS) With B, ch 3 (counts as dc here and throughout), turn, dc in each dc across.

Row 3 With C, repeat Row 2.

Rows 4–26 (28, 30, 34, 36) Repeat Row 2, continuing to work in established stripe pattern.

Fasten off.

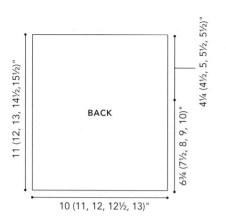

BACK

11 (12, 13, 14½, 15½)"

6¾ (7½, 8, 9, 10)"

4¼ (4½, 5, 5½, 5½)"

10 (11, 12, 12½, 13)"

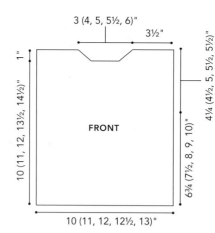

FRONT

3 (4, 5, 5½, 6)"

3½"

1"

10 (11, 12, 13½, 14½)"

6¾ (7½, 8, 9, 10)"

4¼ (4½, 5, 5½, 5½)"

10 (11, 12, 12½, 13)"

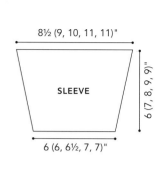

SLEEVE

8½ (9, 10, 11, 11)"

6 (7, 8, 9, 9)"

6 (6, 6½, 7, 7)"

Front

Work as for Back through Row 24 (26, 28, 32, 34).

SHAPE FIRST SHOULDER AND NECK

Row 1 (RS) Ch 3, turn, dc in next 15 dc, hdc in next dc, sc in next dc; leave remaining sts unworked (for neck and second shoulder)—16 dc, 1 hdc, and 1 sc. Fasten off.

Row 2 (WS) Turn, sk first 2 sts, maintaining stripe pattern join yarn with sc in first dc; hdc in next dc, dc in each remaining dc across—1 sc, 1 hdc, and 14 dc. Fasten off.

SHAPE SECOND SHOULDER AND NECK

Row 1 (RS) Sk next 10 (14, 18, 20, 22) unworked sts following first neck edge, join yarn in next st; ch 1, sc in same st as join, hdc in next st, dc in remaining 12 sts—1 sc, 1 hdc, and 16 dc.

Row 2 (WS) Ch 3, turn, dc in next 13 dc, hdc in next dc, sc in next dc; leave last 2 sts unworked—14 dc, 1 hdc, and 1 sc. Fasten off.

Sleeve (make 2)

With A, ch 30 (30, 32, 34, 34).

Row 1 (RS) Dc in 4th ch from hook and each ch across—28 (28, 30, 32, 32) dc.

Rows 2–4 (4, 3, 3, 3) Ch 3, turn, dc in each dc across.

BEGIN SHAPING

Row 5 (5, 4, 4, 4) Ch 3, turn, dc in first dc (increase made), dc in each dc across to last dc, 2 dc in last dc (increase made)—30 (30, 32, 34, 34) dc.

Row 6 (6, 5, 5, 5) Repeat Row 2.

Rows 7 (7, 6, 6, 6)–14 (16, 19, 21, 21) Repeat Rows 5 and 6, 4 (5, 7, 8, 8) more times—38 (40, 46, 50, 50) dc.

Fasten off.

Finishing

NECK EDGING

NOTE: *If you prefer not to use the buttons, sew both shoulder seams, evenly single crochet around the neck edge of the sweater, and fasten off. If you are to use buttons, work as follows:*

Sew right shoulder seam.

Round 1 Join A in first st of unsewn left shoulder seam; ch 1, sc in first 4 dc, [ch 2, sk next 2 dc, sc in next 2 dc] twice (2 buttonholes made), dc in next dc, sc in next dc, evenly sc around entire front and back edge of neck and back shoulder. Fasten off.

REDUCED SAMPLE OF PATTERN

STITCH KEY

⬮ = chain (ch)

† = double crochet (dc)

SLEEVE EDGING

Join A in seam at end of Sleeve, ch 1, sc evenly around cuff edge; join with sl st in first sc. Fasten off. Repeat for second sleeve.

LOWER EDGING

Join A in side seam at lower edge of sweater, ch 1, sc evenly around lower edge; join with sl st in first sc. Fasten off.

Weave in all ends.

ASSEMBLY

Sew two buttons to the back left shoulder seam, aligned with the button holes. Button the front and back pieces together and lay them flat. Measuring across side edges, place a stitch marker 4¼ (4½, 5, 5½, 5½)" (11 [11.5, 12, 14, 14]cm) from each shoulder seam on both the front and back pieces. Mark the center top of each sleeve. With right sides together, align the top corners of each sleeve with the marked stitches on either side of the sweater and the center top of each sleeve with the corresponding shoulder seam. Slip stitch each sleeve to the sweater along the aligned edge. Fold sweater and sleeves in half, with right sides together, and slip stitch the sleeve and side seams together. Turn sweater right side out.

TRY THIS!

Substitute Tahki Yarns *Cotton Classic Lite* in colors #4458 Hot Pink (A), #4532 Pale Lemon (B) and #4449 Bubblegum Pink (C).

sweet daisy sundress

Fingering-weight yarn forms flowing, lightweight fabric that's perfect for spring and summer dresses. Embroidered daisies and a ribbon tie are the girly touches that will make this dress a favorite. Layer it with a cute skirt or slip, or even a pair of bloomers, to complete the look. Whether you crochet it for a special occasion or everyday wear, it's sure to become a family heirloom.

SKILL LEVEL
Intermediate

SIZES	0–6 months	6–12 months	12–18 months	2–3 years	3–4 years
FINISHED CHEST	20" (51cm)	22" (56cm)	24" (61cm)	25½" (65cm)	27" (68.5cm)
FINISHED LENGTH	15¼" (38.5cm)	17" (43cm)	18" (45.5cm)	19½" (49.5cm)	22" (56cm)
MAIN YARN	560 yd (512m)	610 yd (558m)	650 yd (594m)	725 yd (663m)	750 yd (686m)
DETAIL YARN			small amount of 3 contrasting colors		

MATERIALS
560 (610, 650, 725, 750) yards (512 [558, 594, 663, 686]m) of sock yarn: 3 (3, 3, 4, 4) skeins Brown Sheep Company *Cotton Fine*, 80% cotton, 20% wool, 222 yards (204m), 1¾ oz (50g), 3 (3, 3, 4, 4) skeins #CF900 Perry's Primrose for sundress, plus a small amount each #CF210 Tea Rose, #CF100 Cotton Ball, and #CF345 Gold Dust for embroidery **①**

NOTE: *You can use embroidery floss in place of the yarn for the embroidered details.*

Size D-3 (3.25mm) crochet hook, *or size to obtain gauge*

Size E-4 (3.5mm) crochet hook

Yarn needle

3 buttons, ⅜" (9mm) diameter

Sewing needle and thread

1½ yards (1.5m) satin ribbon, ⅜" (9mm) wide

GAUGE
21⅓ sts and 14 rows = 4" (10cm) over hdc with smaller hook.

INSTRUCTIONS
NOTE: *The bodice is worked from the waist up to the shoulders. The skirt is then worked from the lower edge of the bodice down to the hem.*

Bodice (make 2)
With smaller hook, ch 56 (60, 66, 70, 74).

Row 1 (RS) Hdc in 3rd ch from hook (beginning ch does not count as a st) and in each ch across—54 (58, 64, 68, 72) hdc.

Rows 2–4 (6, 6, 8, 10) Ch 2 (does not count as a st), turn, hdc in each hdc across.

SHAPE ARMHOLES
Row 1 Turn, sl st in first 0 (0, 0, 1, 2) hdc, ch 2, hdc2tog, hdc in each hdc across to last 2 (2, 2, 3, 4) hdc, hdc2tog; leave any remaining sts unworked—52 (56, 62, 64, 66) hdc.

Rows 2–7 Ch 2, turn, hdc2tog, hdc in each hdc across to last 2 hdc, hdc2tog—40 (44, 50, 52, 54) hdc.

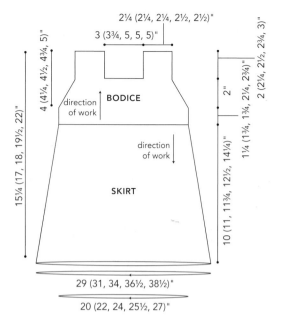

2¼ (2¼, 2¼, 2½, 2½)"
3 (3¾, 5, 5, 5)"
4 (4¼, 4½, 4¾, 5)"
15¼ (17, 18, 19½, 22)"
direction of work
BODICE
2"
2 (2¼, 2½, 2¾, 3)"
1¼ (1¾, 1¾, 2¼, 2¾)"
direction of work
SKIRT
10 (11, 11¾, 12½, 14¼)"
29 (31, 34, 36½, 38½)"
20 (22, 24, 25½, 27)"

SHAPE FIRST SHOULDER AND NECK

Row 8 Ch 2, turn, hdc in next 12 (12, 12, 13, 14) hdc; leave remaining sts unworked (for second shoulder and neck)—12 (12, 12, 13, 14) hdc.

Rows 9–14 (15, 16, 16, 17) Ch 2, turn, hdc in each hdc across.

Fasten off.

SHAPE SECOND SHOULDER AND NECK

Sk next 16 (20, 26, 26, 26) unworked sts following first shoulder, join yarn in next st.

Row 8 Ch 2, hdc in same st as join, hdc in each remaining hdc across—12 (12, 12, 13, 14) hdc.

Rows 9–14 (15, 16, 16, 17) Ch 2, turn, hdc in each hdc across.

Fasten off. Sew bodice pieces together at side seams.

Skirt

NOTE: *The skirt is worked in the round, from the lower edge of the bodice downward. Do not turn at the beginning of the rounds.*

With smaller hook, join yarn in underarm seam on lower edge of bodice.

Round 1 Ch 2, work 108 (116, 128, 136, 144) hdc evenly around lower edge of bodice—108 (116, 128, 136, 144) hdc. Change to larger hook.

Round 2 With larger hook, ch 4 (counts as dc, ch 1 here and throughout), dc in same st as join (beginning V-st made), sk next hdc, *(dc, ch 1, dc) in next hdc (V-st made), sk next hdc; repeat from * around; join with sl st in 3rd ch of beginning ch—54 (58, 64, 68, 72) V-sts.

Round 3 (Sl st, ch 3, 2 dc) in next ch-1 sp, 3 dc in each ch-1 sp around; join with sl st in top of beginning ch—54 (58, 64, 68, 72) 3-dc groups.

Round 4 (Sl st, ch 4, dc) in next dc (center dc of 3-dc group), sk next 2 dc, *(dc, ch 1, dc) in next dc, sk next 2 dc; repeat from * around; join with sl st in 3rd ch of beginning ch.

Round 5 Repeat Round 3.

Rounds 6–23 (25, 27, 29, 33) Repeat last 2 rounds 9 (10, 11, 12, 14) more times.

Round 24 (26, 28, 30, 34) *work (Dc, ch 2, sl st, ch 2, 2 dc, ch 2, sl st, ch 2, dc) in sp between next two 3-dc groups, sl st in sp between next two 3-dc groups (half flower made); repeat from * around; join with sl st top of beginning ch of previous round—27 (29, 32, 34, 36) half flowers.

Fasten off.

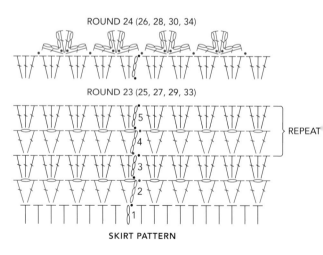

ROUND 24 (26, 28, 30, 34)
ROUND 23 (25, 27, 29, 33)
5
4
3
2
1
REPEAT

SKIRT PATTERN

STITCH KEY

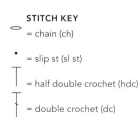

= chain (ch)

= slip st (sl st)

= half double crochet (hdc)

= double crochet (dc)

LEFT ARMHOLE, SHOULDER, AND NECK EDGING

Determine which side of the dress will be the front, and mark the front bodice with a stitch marker. Sew the right shoulder seam. Do not sew the left shoulder seam, as buttons will be attached later to make the dress easy to get on and off. With the smaller hook, join the yarn in the top back corner of the left armhole (unseamed shoulder).

Round 1 Ch 1, work sc evenly around entire armhole, across front shoulder, around neck edge, and across back shoulder, working 3 sc in each outer corner of shoulder; join with sl st in first sc.

Round 2 *Ch 4, sk next sc, sl st in next sc; repeat from * around armhole and across front shoulder.

NOTE: *Ch-4 sps across front shoulder will serve as button loops.*

Fasten off.

RIGHT ARMHOLE EDGING

With smaller hook, join yarn in shoulder seam of right armhole.

Round 1 Ch 1, work sc evenly around entire armhole; join with sl st in first sc.

Round 2 *Ch 4, sk next sc, sl st in next sc; repeat from * around.

Fasten off.

Finishing

Weave in all ends. Sew three small buttons on the top back of the left shoulder, opposite the three ch-4 button loops. Using small amounts of contrasting yarn (or embroidery floss), embroider daisies on the front bodice of dress (instructions at right).

Beginning in the center front of the skirt, thread a ribbon in and out of the V-stitches from Round 2 of the skirt. Tie a bow and trim the ribbon ends.

> **TIP** The plain bodice of this dress lends itself to embellishment. Decorate it with your own embroidered design, a monogram, or even crocheted or fabric flowers.

HOW TO EMBROIDER LAZY DAISIES

Weave the yarn through about 1" of stitches on the wrong side of the front bodice and leave a long tail to weave in later. Push your needle and yarn through to the right side of the bodice where you'd like the center of the daisy to be. **(a)** Form a small ½" (13mm) loop with the yarn; this will be the petal. Reinsert the needle in the same spot where the yarn originally came through, then bring it back through to the bodice front just inside of the petal loop. **(b)** Reinsert the needle on the outside edge of the petal loop and pull the yarn through to hold the loop in place. Repeat to make 5 petals, or as many as desired, for each flower. Weave in all ends.

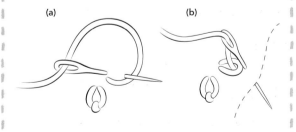

(a) (b)

cozy crawlers leg warmers

You might think of leg warmers as a fad from the '80s, but on babies and toddlers they're perfect for layering—and convenience! The hip alternative to pants, leg warmers keep your baby warm without getting in the way of diaper changes or potty training, plus they provide cushioning for babies who are learning to crawl. Use up leftover bits of sock yarn to make a truly wild pair, or try a solid color for an easy-to-layer look.

SKILL LEVEL
Intermediate

SIZES	6–12 months	12–18 months	2 years
FINISHED CIRCUMFERENCE	8" (20.5cm)	8½" (21.5cm)	9" (23cm)
FINISHED LENGTH	8½" (21.5cm)	9¼" (23.5cm)	10" (25.5cm)
COLOR A	120 yd (110m)	160 yd (147m)	190 yd (174m)
COLOR B	120 yd (110m)	160 yd (147m)	190 yd (174m)

MATERIALS
240 (320, 380) yards (220 [294, 348]m) of sock yarn: 1 skein of Knit Picks *Stroll Hand Painted Sock Yarn*, 75% superwash merino wool, 25% nylon, 462 yards (424m), 3½ oz (100g), Playtime (A). 1 skein of Knit Picks *Stroll Sock Yarn*, 75% superwash merino wool, 25% nylon, 231 yards (212m), 1¾ oz (50g), Buckskin (B)

Size D-3 (3.25mm) crochet hook, *or size to obtain gauge*

Yarn needle

2 buttons, ½" (13mm) diameter (optional)

GAUGE
22 sts and 16 rows = 4" (10cm) over extended single crochet.

SPECIAL STITCHES
Foundation Double Crochet (Fdc): Advanced Stitches, page 151.

Extended Single Crochet (esc): Insert hook in next stitch, yarn over and draw up a loop. Yarn over and draw the loop through 1 loop on your hook, yarn over again and draw the loop through the remaining 2 loops on your hook.

Extended Single Crochet Decrease (esc dec): (Insert hook in next stitch, yarn over and draw up a loop) twice, draw last loop on hook through second loop on hook. Yarn over and draw the loop through remaining 2 loops on hook.

INSTRUCTIONS

NOTE: *Each leg warmer is worked in joined rounds, beginning at the top. Do not turn at the beginning of the rounds. The colors are changed regularly. When changing to a new color, do not fasten off the old color. Instead, carry the old color up the WS (inside) of the legging. For seamless color changes, change colors at the last yarn over of the last stitch in the old color before joining each round.*

Leg Warmer (make 2)

Round 1 (RS) With B, Fdc 44 (46, 50); join with sl st in first Fdc—44 (46, 50) sts.

Rounds 2–4 Ch 2 (does not count as a st), *FPdc in next st, BPdc in next st; repeat from * around; join with sl st in first FPdc. Join A in same st as join.

Rounds 5 and 6 With A, ch 2 (counts as first esc here and throughout), esc in each st around; join with sl st in top of beginning ch.

Round 7 Pick up B, repeat Round 5.

Rounds 8–25 (28, 31) Repeat last 3 rounds 6 (7, 8) times.

Rounds 26 (29, 32) and 27 (30, 33) Repeat Rounds 5 and 6.

Round 28 (31, 34) With B, ch 2, esc in next 8 (10, 7) sts, *esc dec, esc in next 9 (9, 8) sts; repeat from * around; esc dec; join with sl st in top of beginning ch—40 (42, 45) sts.

Rounds 29 (32, 35)–31 (34, 37) Repeat Rounds 5–7.

Rounds 32 (35, 38) and 33 (36, 39) Repeat Rounds 5 and 6.

Round 34 (37, 40) With B, ch 2, esc in next 7 (9, 6) sts, *esc dec, esc in next 8 (8, 7) sts; repeat from * around, esc dec; join with sl st in top of beginning ch—36 (38, 40) sts.

Rounds 35 (38, 41)–37 (40, 43) Repeat Rounds 5–7.

Round 38 (41, 44) With A, ch 2 (does not count as a stitch), *FPdc around next st, BPdc around next st; repeat from * around; join with sl st in first FPdc.

Fasten off.

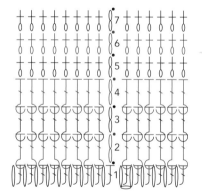

REDUCED SAMPLE OF PATTERN STITCH

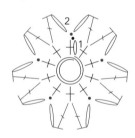

FLOWER

STITCH KEY

⌒ = chain (ch)

• = slip st (sl st)

+ = single crochet (sc)

= extended single crochet (esc)

= foundation double crochet (Fdc)

= double crochet (dc)

= Front Post double crochet (FPdc)

= Back Post double crochet (BPdc)

= adjustable ring

Flower (make 2, optional)

With A, make an adjustable ring.

Round 1 (RS) Ch 1, 10 sc in ring; join with sl st in first sc—10 sc.

Round 2 Ch 1, 2 dc in next sc, [ch 1, sl st in next sc, ch 1, 2 dc in next sc] 4 times, ch 1; join with sl st in first sc of Round 1—5 petals.

Fasten off.

Finishing

On each leg warmer, sew the edges of the foundation row together. Flatten the leg warmer so that the seam is in the middle of one side. Sew a flower and a button (optional) to the center top of the other side of the leg warmer (opposite the seam). Weave in all ends.

TIP Customize these leg warmers to fit any size child. Increase the length of the leg warmers by adding more rows of the stripe pattern before the decrease rows—add 4 rows for each inch (2.5cm) of length. To increase width, multiply the desired circumference in inches (cm) by 5½ (the number of stitches per inch [2.5cm] according to gauge) to determine the number of foundation stitches to crochet. If necessary, round this number down to an even number to maintain the stitch pattern.

striped yoke cardigan

This handsome sweater is a classic design for any child's wardrobe. Patch pockets attached with contrasting slip stitches and chunky buttons make it stand out. The simple pattern lends itself to variation—you can make a closet full of options for your child by using fancy stitches around the yoke of the sweater, changing the stripe pattern, or crocheting a frilly trim around the button band.

SKILL LEVEL
Easy

SIZES	0–6 months	6–12 months	1–2 years	3–4 years
FINISHED CHEST	20½" (52cm)	23" (58.5cm)	25" (63.5cm)	27½" (70cm)
FINISHED LENGTH	11" (28cm)	12" (30.5cm)	12¾" (32.5cm)	14¼" (36cm)
COLOR A	260 yd (238m)	310 yd (284m)	360 yd (330m)	430 yd (393m)
COLORS B AND C each	45 yd (41m)	55 yd (50m)	65 yd (60m)	85 yd (78m)

MATERIALS
350 (420, 490, 600) yards (343 [384, 448, 549]m) of worsted-weight yarn: 5 (5, 6, 7) skeins Berroco *Pure Merino Heather*, 100% merino wool, 92 yards (85m), 1¾ oz (50g), 3 (4, 4, 5) skeins #8613 Winter Chocolate (A), and 1 (1, 1, 1) skein each #8619 Mowbray Beige (B) and #8611 Pesto Genovese (C) (4)

Size H-8 (5mm) crochet hook, *or size to obtain gauge*

Yarn needle

5 (5, 5, 6) buttons, ¾" (19mm) diameter

GAUGE
14 sts and 10 rows = 4" (10cm) over hdc;

14 sts and 8 rows = 4" (10cm) over dc.

INSTRUCTIONS
NOTE: *This sweater is worked in rows from the top down. Row 2 is the RS for sizes 0–6 months and 1–2 years, Row 1 is the RS for sizes 6–12 months and 3–4 years.*

Yoke
With A, ch 46, (49, 55, 58).

Row 1 Sc in 2nd ch from hook, sc in next ch, 2 sc in next ch, [sc in next 2 ch, 2 sc in next ch] 14 (15, 17, 18) times—60 (64, 72, 76) sc.

Row 2 Ch 2 (counts as hdc here and throughout), turn, hdc in next 8 (9, 10, 11) sc, (hdc, ch 1, hdc) in next sc, hdc in next 10 (10, 12, 12) sc, (hdc, ch 1, hdc) in next sc, hdc in next 18 (20, 22, 24) sc, (hdc, ch 1, hdc) in next sc, hdc in next 10 (10, 12, 12) sc, (hdc, ch 1, hdc) in next sc, hdc in remaining 9 (10, 11, 12) sc; change to B in last st—64 (68, 76, 80) hdc.

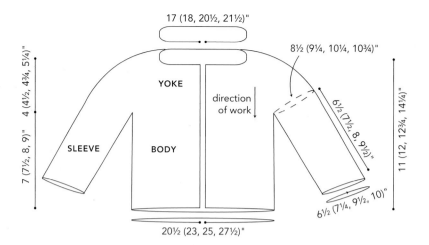

17 (18, 20½, 21½)"

8½ (9¼, 10¼, 10¾)"

YOKE

direction of work

SLEEVE   BODY

7 (7½, 8, 9)"

4 (4½, 4¾, 5¼)"

11 (12, 12¾, 14¼)"

6½ (7½, 8, 9½)"

6½ (7¼, 9½, 10)"

20½ (23, 25, 27½)"

Row 3 Ch 2 (counts as hdc here and throughout), turn, *hdc in each hdc to next ch-1 sp, (hdc, ch 1, hdc) in next ch-1 sp; repeat from * 3 more times, hdc in each hdc to end; change to C in last st—72 (76, 84, 88) hdc.

Row 4 Repeat Row 3; change to A in last st—80 (84, 92, 96) hdc.

Row 5 Repeat Row 3; change to B in last st—88 (92, 100, 104) hdc.

Row 6 Repeat Row 3; change to C in last st—96 (100, 108, 112) hdc.

Row 7 Repeat Row 3; change to A in last st—104 (108, 116, 120) hdc. Fasten off C.

Row 8 Repeat Row 3; change to B in last st—112 (116, 124, 128) hdc.

Row 9 Repeat Row 3; change to A in last st—120 (124, 132, 136) hdc. Fasten off B.

Row 10 Repeat Row 3—128 (132, 140, 144) dc.

Sizes 6–12 months (1–2 years, 3–4 years) only
Row 11 Repeat Row 3—140 (148, 152) hdc.

Sizes 1–2 years (3–4 years) only
Row 12 Repeat Row 3—156 (160) hdc.

Size 3–4 years only
Row 13 Repeat Row 3—168 hdc.

DIVIDE FOR BODY AND ARMHOLES (all sizes)
Row 1 (WS) With A, ch 3 (counts as dc here and throughout), turn, *dc in each hdc to last hdc before next ch-1 sp, dc2tog over next hdc and ch-1 sp, sk next 28 (30, 34, 36) hdc (armhole made), dc2tog over ch-1 sp and next hdc*, dc in each hdc to last hdc before next ch-1 sp, repeat from * to *, dc in each hdc to end—72 (80, 88, 96) dc.

Rows 2–14 (15, 16, 18) Ch 3, turn, dc in each dc across.

Fasten off.

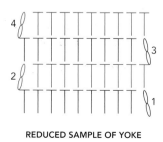

4
3
2
1

REDUCED SAMPLE OF YOKE

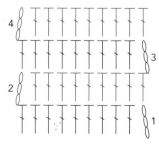

4
3
2
1

REDUCED SAMPLE OF BODY

STITCH KEY

⬭ = chain (ch)

⊤ = half double crochet (hdc)

⊥ = double crochet (dc)

Sleeves (all sizes)

NOTE: *Although sleeves are worked in the round, turn at the beginning of each round so that the RS and WS rows match up with the body of the garment.*

Round 1 (RS) Join A in ch-1 sp of underarm; ch 3, dc in next ch-1 sp, dc in each hdc around; join with sl st in top of beginning ch—30 (32, 36, 38) dc.

Rounds 2–4 Ch 3, turn, dc in each dc around; join with sl st in top of beginning ch.

Round 5 Ch 3, turn, dc in next 7 dc, dc2tog, [dc in next 8 dc, dc2tog] twice, dc in remaining 0 (2, 6, 8) dc; join with sl st in top of beginning ch—27 (29, 33, 35) dc.

Rounds 6–9 Repeat Round 2.

Round 10 Ch 3, turn, dc in next 3 dc, dc2tog, [dc in next 4 dc, dc2tog] 3 (3, 4, 4) times, dc in remaining 3 (5, 3, 5) dc; join with sl st in top of beginning ch—23 (25, 28, 30) dc.

Rounds 11–13 (15, 16, 19) Repeat Round 2; change to B in last st of last row.

Round 14 (16, 17, 20) Ch 1, sc in each dc around; join with sl st in first sc.

Fasten off.

Pockets (make 2)

With A, ch 12 (12, 14, 16).

Row 1 (WS) Dc in 4th ch from hook and each ch across—10 (10, 12, 14) dc.

Rows 2–5 (5, 5, 7) Ch 3, turn, dc in each dc across.

Row 6 (6, 6, 8) Turn, sk first 2 dc, 3 dc in next dc, dc in each dc across to last 2 dc, 3 dc in next dc, sl st in last st of row—10 (10, 12, 14) dc.

Edging Round (RS) Do not turn, ch 1, sc evenly along side edge, top and opposite side edge of pocket, stopping just before last row of second side edge; join with a sl st in the first dc of Row 6. Fasten off.

Finishing

BUTTON BAND

With RS facing, join A in corner of Left Front (for boys) or Right Front (for girls), to work along front edge.

Row 1 Ch 1, evenly work 40 (42, 46, 50) sc along front edge—40 (42, 46, 50) sc.

Row 2 Ch 1, turn, sc in first 3 (4, 4, 4) sc, ch 2, sk next 2 sc (buttonhole made), *sc in next 6 (6, 7, 6) sc, ch 2, sk next 2 sc; repeat from * 3 (3, 3, 4) times more, sc in remaining 3 (4, 4, 4) sc—30 (32, 36, 38) sc and 5 (5, 5, 6) buttonholes.

Row 3 Ch 1, turn, sc in each sc and ch across—40 (42, 46, 50) sc.

Fasten off.

FRONT EDGING

With RS facing, join yarn A in corner of Right Front (for boys) or Left Front (for girls), to work along front edge.

Row 1 Ch 1, work 40 (42, 46, 50) sc evenly along front edge—40 (42, 46, 50) sc.

Fasten off.

POCKET EDGING

Pin each pocket in place on the sweater front. With B, working through both the pocket and sweater layers, slip stitch around the side and lower edges of the pocket (Surface Slip Stitch, page 151). Cut the yarn, leaving an 18" (45.5cm) tail, and pull it through the sweater layer (but not through the pocket). Continue to slip stitch around upper edge of pocket to complete the contrast edging.

SWEATER EDGING

Join B in the lower front corner to work across lower edge.

Round 1 Ch 1, work sc evenly across the lower edge of the sweater; do not fasten off, sl st evenly up the front edge, around the neck and down the opposite front edge of the sweater; join with sl st in first sc. Fasten off.

Sew buttons in place along the front edge directly across from the buttonholes.

Weave in all ends.

SOCK IT TO ME SWEATER VEST

This cute wardrobe staple is worked from side to side in two pieces to form a faux rib pattern, then edged with post stitch cables in a solid color. The best part? You can make it with just a little more yarn than it takes to make a pair of socks. The fun colors and lightweight, durable fibers found in most sock yarns make them an excellent choice for crocheting kids' garments.

SKILL LEVEL
Intermediate

SIZES	0–6 months	6–12 months	12–18 months	2 years	3–4 years
FINISHED CHEST	19½" (49.5cm)	22" (56cm)	24" (61cm)	25" (63.5cm)	27" (68.5cm)
FINISHED LENGTH (including ribbing)	11¼" (28.5cm)	12" (30.5cm)	13" (33cm)	13¼" (33.5cm)	14¼" (36cm)
COLOR A	430 yd (394m)	430 yd (394m)	430 yd (394m)	645 yd (591m)	645 yd (591m)
COLOR B	100 yd (91m)	100 yd (91m)	100 yd (91m)	130 yd (119m)	130 yd (119m)

MATERIALS
530 (530, 530, 775, 775) yards (486 [486, 486, 711, 711]m) of sock yarn: 3 (3, 3, 4, 4) skeins Lorna's Laces *Shepherd Sock*, 80% superwash wool, 20% nylon, 215 yards (197m), 2 oz (57g), 2 (2, 2, 3, 3) skeins Franklin's Panopticon (A), 1 (1, 1, 1, 1) skein #36NS Chocolate (B) (**1**)

Size D-3 (3.25mm) crochet hook, *or size to obtain gauge*

Yarn needle

GAUGE
22½ sts and 13½ rows = 4" (10cm) over pattern stitch.

PATTERN STITCH
Alternating Rows of Hdc/Dc: Worked over any number of sts.

Row 1 (WS) Dc in 4th ch from hook (beginning ch counts as first dc) and in each ch across.

Row 2 Ch 2 (does not count as a st), turn, working in back loops only, hdc in each st across.

Row 3 Ch 3 (counts as first dc here and throughout), turn, dc in each st across.

Repeat Rows 2 and 3 for pattern stitch.

SPECIAL STITCHES
Front Post Double Crochet (FPdc), Back Post Double Crochet (BPdc) and Foundation Double Crochet (Fdc): Advanced Stitches, pages 151 and 152.

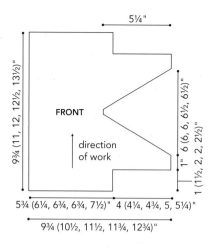

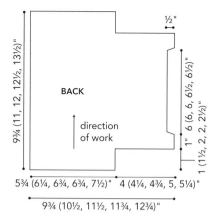

INSTRUCTIONS

NOTE: *The rows of the front and back are worked lengthwise, and the pieces are worked from one side edge across to the other side edge.*

Front

With A, ch 34 (36, 40, 44, 48).

Row 1 (WS) Dc in 4th ch from hook (beginning ch counts as dc) and in each ch across—32 (34, 38, 38, 42) dc.

Row 2 (RS) Ch 2 (does not count as a st), turn, working in back loops only, hdc in each dc across.

Row 3 Ch 3 (counts as first dc here and throughout), turn, dc in each hdc across.

Repeat last 2 rows 0 (1, 2, 2, 3) more times.

Row 4 (6, 8, 8, 10) Ch 24 (26, 28, 30, 32), turn, hdc in 3rd ch from hook and in each ch across, working in back loops only, hdc in each dc across—54 (58, 64, 66, 72) hdc.

Row 5 (7, 9, 9, 11) Ch 3, turn, dc in each hdc across.

Row 6 (8, 10, 10, 12) Ch 2, turn, working in back loops only, hdc in each dc across.

SHAPE NECK

Row 7 (9, 11, 11, 13) Ch 3, turn, dc in each hdc to last 3 hdc; leave last 3 hdc unworked—51 (55, 61, 63, 69) hdc.

Row 8 (10, 12, 12, 14) Turn, sl st over first 4 sts, ch 2, working in back loops only, hdc in same st as last sl st, dc in each st across—48 (52, 58, 60, 66) hdc.

Row 9 (11, 13, 13, 15) Repeat Row 9 (11, 11, 13)—45 (49, 55, 57, 63) dc.

Rows 10 (12, 14, 14, 16)–13 (15, 17, 17, 19) Repeat Rows 8 (10, 12, 12, 14) and 9 (11, 13, 13, 15) twice—33 (37, 43, 45, 51) dc.

Row 14 (16, 18, 18, 20) Repeat Row 8 (10, 12, 12, 14)—30 (34, 40, 42, 48) hdc.

Row 15 (17, 19, 19, 21) Ch 3, turn, dc in each hdc across to last 2 hdc; leave last 2 hdc unworked—28 (32, 38, 40, 46) dc.

Row 16 (18, 20, 20, 22) Turn, sl st in first 3 sts, ch 2, working in back loops only, hdc in same st as last sl st, hdc in each dc across—26 (30, 36, 38, 44) hdc.

Row 17 (19, 21, 21, 23) Ch 3, turn, dc in each hdc across to last hdc; leave last hdc unworked—25 (29, 35, 37, 43) dc.

Sizes 2–3 years (3–4 years) only
Row 22 (24) Ch 2, turn, hdc in each dc across.

Row 23 (25) Ch 2, turn, hdc in each dc across.

All sizes
Row 18 (20, 22, 24, 26) Ch 3, turn, hdc in 3rd ch from hook, working in back loops only, hdc in each dc across—26 (30, 36, 38, 44) hdc.

Row 19 (21, 23, 25, 27) Ch 3, turn, dc in each hdc across, work 2 Fdc—28 (32, 38, 40, 46) sts.

Row 20 (22, 24, 26, 28) Ch 4, turn, hdc in 3rd ch from hook and next ch, working in back loops only, hdc in each dc across—30 (34, 40, 42, 48) hdc.

Row 21 (23, 25, 27, 29) Ch 3, turn, dc in each hdc across, work 3 Fdc—33 (37, 43, 45, 51) sts.

Row 22 (24, 26, 28, 30) Ch 5, turn, hdc in 3rd ch from hook and in next 2 ch, working in back loops only, hdc in each dc across—36 (40, 46, 48, 54) hdc.

Rows 23 (25, 27, 29, 31)–28 (30, 32, 34, 36) Repeat last 2 rows three times—54 (58, 64, 66, 72) sts.

Row 29 (31, 33, 35, 37) Ch 3, turn, dc in each hdc across.

Row 30 (32, 34, 36, 38) Ch 2, turn, hdc in each dc across.

Row 31 (33, 35, 37, 39) Ch 3, turn, dc in first 31 (33, 37, 37, 41) hdc; leave remaining sts unworked—32 (34, 38, 38, 42) dc.

Row 32 (34, 36, 38, 40) Ch 2, turn, hdc in each dc across.

Row 33 (35, 37, 39, 41) Ch 3, turn, dc in each hdc across.

Repeat last 2 rows 0 (1, 2, 2, 3) more times.

Fasten off.

Back

Work the Back the same as the Front through Row 8 (10, 12, 12, 14)—48 (52, 58, 60, 66) hdc.

Row 9 (11, 13, 13, 15) Ch 3, turn, dc in each st across.

Row 10 (12, 14, 14, 16) Ch 2, turn, working in back loops only, hdc in each dc across.

Rows 11 (13, 15, 15, 17)–26 (28, 30, 32, 34) Repeat last 2 rows 8 (8, 8, 10, 10) more times.

Row 27 (29, 31, 33, 35) Ch 3, turn, dc in each hdc across, work 3 Fdc—51 (55, 61, 63, 69) sts.

Row 28 (30, 32, 34, 36) Ch 5, turn, hdc in 3rd ch from hook and in next 2 ch, working in back loops only, hdc in each dc across—54 (58, 64, 66, 72) sts.

Row 29 (31, 33, 35, 37) Ch 3, turn, dc in each hdc across.

Row 30 (32, 34, 36, 38) Ch 2, turn, hdc in each dc across.

Row 31 (33, 35, 37, 39) Ch 3, turn, dc in first 31 (33, 37, 37, 41) hdc; leave remaining sts unworked—32 (34, 38, 38, 42) dc.

Row 32 (34, 36, 38, 40) Ch 2, turn, hdc in each dc across.

Row 33 (35, 37, 39, 41) Ch 3, turn, dc in each hdc across.

Repeat last 2 rows 0 (1, 2, 2, 3) more times.

Fasten off.

Finishing

Sew the shoulder seams and the side seams.

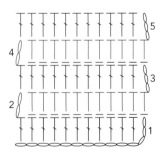

REDUCED SAMPLE OF PATTERN STITCH ALTERNATING ROWS OF HDC/DC

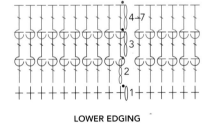

LOWER EDGING

STITCH KEY

⌒ = chain (ch)

• = slip st (sl st)

+ = single crochet (sc)

T = half double crochet (hdc)

T = double crochet (dc)

T = Front Post double crochet (FPdc)

T = Back Post double crochet (BPdc)

— = worked in back loop only

NECK EDGING

Round 1 With right side facing, join A in center back edge, ch 1, work sc evenly around entire neck edge, working 1 sc in the side of each hdc row and 2 sc in the side of each dc row; work 1 sc in each unworked sc and sl st across left neck shaping, skipping the last sc in each row; work 1 sc in each unworked sc and sl st across right neck shaping, skipping the first sc in each row; join with sl st in first sc. Fasten off.

Round 2 Join B in same st as join, ch 3, dc in each sc around to 2 sts before center front neck st, (dc2tog) twice, dc in each remaining sc around; join with sl st in top of beginning ch. Fasten off.

ARMHOLE EDGING

Round 1 With right side facing, join A in seam at underarm, ch 1, sc evenly around armhole edge; join with sl st in first sc. Fasten off.

Round 2 With right side facing, join B in same st as join, ch 3, dc in each sc around; join with sl st in top of beginning ch. Fasten off.

LOWER EDGING

Round 1 With right side facing, join A in center lower edge of Back, ch 1, sc evenly around the edge, making sure that you work an even number of sts; join with sl st in first sc. Fasten off.

Round 2 With right side facing, join B in same st as join, ch 3, dc in each sc around; join with sl st in top of beginning ch.

Round 3 Ch 2 (does not count as a st here and throughout), *FPdc in next dc, BPdc in next dc; repeat from * around; join with sl st in first FPdc.

Rounds 4–7 Ch 2, *FPdc in next FPdc, BPdc in next BPdc; repeat from * around; join with sl st in first FPdc.

Fasten off. Weave in all ends.

TIP Save your extra yarn when you complete this project. When your child outgrows the length of the vest, crochet extra edging rows along the bottom to make it wearable for a few more months.

STRAWBERRY PATCH PARTY FROCK

Combine a crocheted bodice with a bold fabric skirt to make this summery sundress. Stitch the motifs in as many colors as you like—each square uses only a touch of yarn. The motifs are joined as you go, so it's easy to keep all of the pieces together, and you're saved from having to seam them when you're done crocheting.

SKILL LEVEL
Intermediate

SIZES	3–9 months	12–24 months	3–4 years
FINISHED CHEST	21" (53.5cm)	24" (61cm)	27" (68.5cm)
FINISHED LENGTH	17" (43cm)	18" (45.5cm)	20" (51cm)
COLOR A	100 yd (92m)	110 yd (100m)	170 yd (156m)
COLORS B, C, AND D	30 yd (27m) each	35 yd (32m) each	50 yd (46m) each

MATERIALS
190 (215, 320) yards (187 [197, 283]m) of sportweight yarn: 4 (4, 5) skeins Debbie Bliss *Baby Cashmerino*, 55% merino wool, 33% microfiber, 12% cashmere, 137 yards (126m), 1¾ oz (50g), 1 (1, 2) skeins in #26 Sea Foam (A), and 1 skein each in #2 Spring Grass (B), #7 Magenta (C), and #6 Pink (D) 🄫

Size D-3 (3.25mm) crochet hook (for motifs), *or size to obtain gauge*

Size F-5 (3.75mm) crochet hook (for edging)

Yarn needle

½ (½, ¾) yard (0.5 [0.5, 0.75]m) printed cotton fabric (for skirt)

One heart-shaped button, ⅝" (15mm) diameter

Large sheet of gridded sewing pattern paper, or kraft paper (to make skirt template)

Ruler

Sewing machine (optional)

Sewing needle and thread

Iron

GAUGE
One completed motif measures 1½" (3.8cm) square.

SPECIAL STITCH
Motif Join (MJ): With loop of working motif still on hook, insert hook into corresponding ch-3 sp on neighboring motif, ch 1 around ch-3 sp of joining motif, then continue to follow pattern on working motif.

NOTE: *The letter in each motif indicates the color to be used to work Round 1.*

Size 3–9 months (30 motifs)

D	B	C	D	B	C	D
	C	D	B	C	D	
	D	BODICE			B	
	C				C	
	D	Front			B	
	B	C	D	B	C	
B	C	D	B	C	D	B

← Do not join here.

3¾" 5¼"
10½"
7½"
4½"

Size 12–24 months (36 motifs)

D	B	C	D	B	C	D	B
	C	D	B	C	D	B	
	D	BODICE				C	
	B					D	
	C					B	
	D	Front				C	
	B	C	D	B	C	D	
B	C	D	B	C	D	B	C

← Do not join here.

4½" 6"
12"
9"
6"

Size 3–4 years (52 motifs)

C	D	B	C	D	B	C	D	B
	B	C	D	B	C	D	B	
	C	D	B	C	D	B	C	
	D	BODICE					D	
	B						B	
	C	Front					C	
	D	B	C	D	B	C	D	
	B	C	D	B	C	D	B	
B	C	D	B	C	D	B	C	D

← Do not join here.

5¼" 6¾"
13½"
10½"
7½"

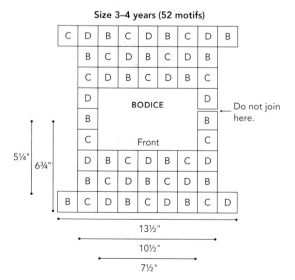

Bodice

NOTE: *Bodice is made from square motifs, joined while working the second round. Refer to the assembly diagram at left for the number and placement of motifs.*

FIRST MOTIF

With smaller hook and B, C, or D, make an adjustable ring.

Round 1 (RS) Ch 3 (counts as dc here and throughout), 2 dc in ring, ch 1, [3 dc in ring, ch 1] 3 times; join with sl st in top of beginning ch—12 dc. Fasten off.

Round 2 Join A with sl st in any ch-1 sp, ch 1, (sc, ch 3, sc) in same ch-1 sp (corner made), ch 3, sk next 3 dc, [(sc, ch 3, sc) in next ch-1 sp (corner made), ch 3, sk next 3 dc] 3 times; join with sl st in first sc—8 ch-3 sps.

NEXT MOTIF (make and join 29 [35, 51])

NOTE: *Make a total of 30 (36, 52) motifs (including the first motif), 10 (12, 18) with B as Round 1 color, 10 (12, 17) each with C and D as Round 1 color.*

Work the same as for the First Motif through Round 1. Refer to the assembly diagram to determine the placement and center color of each subsequent motif, then work the appropriate joining round (to join across one side edge, or across two sides edges of neighboring motifs). Take care to leave one edge of the squares near the top left shoulder un-joined so that a button can be added. (For sizes 3–9 months and 3–4 years, the button will need to be slightly below the shoulder seam, since the squares do not meet exactly at the shoulder). Be sure to join the side edges forming the armholes.

Motifs Joined Across One Side Edge

Round 2 Join A in any ch-1 sp, ch 1, (sc, ch 3, sc) in same ch-1 sp (corner made), ch 3, sk next 3 dc; (sc, ch 1, MJ, ch 1, sc) in next ch-1 sp (corner joined), ch 1, MJ, ch 1 (side joined), sk next 3 dc, (sc, ch 1, MJ, ch 1, sc) in next ch-1 sp (corner joined), ch 3, sk next 3 dc, (sc, ch 3, sc) in next ch-1 sp (corner made), ch 3, sk last 3 dc; join with sl st in first sc—8 ch-3 sps.

Motifs Joined Across Two Side Edges

Round 2 Join A in any ch-1 sp, ch 1, (sc, ch 3, sc) in same ch-1 sp (corner made), ch 3, sk next 3 dc; (sc, ch 1, MJ, ch 1, sc) in next ch-1 sp (corner joined), [ch 1, MJ, ch 1 (side joined), sk next 3 dc, (sc, ch 1, MJ, ch 1, sc) in next ch-1 sp (corner joined)] twice, ch 3, sk last 3 dc; join with sl st in first sc—8 ch-3 sps.

Round 1 Ch 1, work 8 sc evenly spaced across top edge of strap, work sc evenly spaced around neck edge, around edges of un-joined back strap, and around left armhole edge; join with sl st in first sc.

Row 2 Do not turn, continue to work across top of front un-joined strap; ch 1, sc in next 3 sc, ch 2, sk next 2 sc (buttonhole made), sc in next 3 sc—6 sc.

Fasten off. Sew the button to the back of the un-joined strap, directly across from the buttonhole.

With the right side of the bodice facing and the larger hook, join A in any ch-3 sp of the right armhole, ch 1, work sc evenly spaced around the armhole; join with sl st in first sc. Fasten off. Weave in all ends.

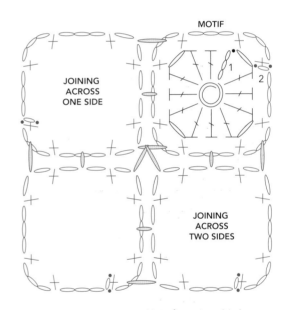

MOTIF

JOINING ACROSS ONE SIDE

JOINING ACROSS TWO SIDES

STITCH KEY

⌒ = chain (ch)

• = slip st (sl st)

+ = single crochet (sc)

⊤ = double crochet (dc)

◎ = adjustable ring

⬭ = Motif Join

LOWER EDGING

With the right side of the bodice facing and the larger hook, join A in any ch-3 sp along the lower edge.

Round 1 Ch 1, work sc evenly spaced around the lower edge, working 3 sc in each side ch-3 sp and 2 sc in each corner ch-3 sp (on either side of join between motifs); join with sl st in first sc. Be sure to work an odd number of single crochet stitches.

Round 2 *Ch 3, sk next sc, sl st in next sc; repeat from * around; join with sl st in first sc of Round 1.

NECK AND ARMHOLE EDGING

With the right side of the bodice facing and the larger hook, join A in the corner ch-3 sp of the un-joined front strap to work across the top of the strap toward the neck.

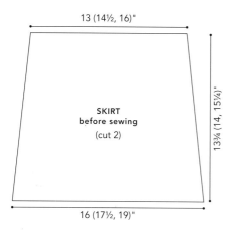

13 (14½, 16)"

13¾ (14, 15¼)"

SKIRT
before sewing
(cut 2)

16 (17½, 19)"

Assemble the Skirt

Cut a piece of pattern paper to the following dimensions
for each size:

3–9 months	16" (40.5cm) wide x 13¾" (35cm) long
12–18 months	17½" (44.5cm) wide x 14" (35.5cm) long
3–4 years	19" (48.5cm) wide x 15¼" (38.5cm) long

Along one widthwise edge of the pattern paper, make
a mark 1½" (3.8cm) in from each edge. Draw a line
from each mark to the corner of the opposite widthwise
edge, creating a slightly flared trapezoid shape (see skirt
schematic). Cut out the shape and use it as a template to
cut two pieces of fabric.

Place the two fabric pieces together so that the right
sides of each piece face each other and the wrong side
of the fabric is facing you. Leaving a ½" (13mm) seam
allowance, sew down each angled side edge and press
the seam open.

Turn the skirt inside out. Fold the lower (wider) edge
under 1" (25mm) and press the fold. Turn the raw edge
of the fold under ½" (13mm) (encasing the raw edge) and
press. Sew the seam along the inner fold. Repeat this
process on the top raw edge of the skirt.

Set your sewing machine, if using, to the longest stitch
length (the basting stitch). Starting about 2" (5cm) in from
one side edge, baste across the top, front edge of the
skirt, ending again about 2" (5cm) from the opposite side
edge. Leave the thread ends long and do NOT backstitch
at the beginning or end of the seam. Pull the top thread
of each side of the basting stitch to gather the fabric.
Gather the fabric until it measures 10½ (12, 13½)" (26.5
[30.5, 34.5]cm) across the top edge, then tie the thread
ends into knots. Repeat this process across the top, back
edge of the skirt.

Pin the bodice to the top, gathered edge of the skirt,
overlapping the lower edge of the bodice with the top
edge of the skirt by about ¼" (6mm). Hand sew the
bodice in place.

TIP   For extra coverage along the bodice, add
an edging to the neck opening, following the same
instructions as for the Lower Edging.

cutie patootie pants

These warm wool pants will keep your baby cozy and protected from leaks. Wool can absorb up to a third of its weight in liquid without feeling wet, making it a perfect fiber choice for soakers and pants. This pattern is worked from the top down, and the roomy fit is designed to accommodate cloth diapers. To customize the fit, try the pants on your baby as you go to make changes to the rise and length of the pants as directed in the pattern.

SKILL LEVEL
Intermediate

SIZES	0–6 months	6–12 months	12–18 months	2 years	3–4 years
FINISHED WAIST (unstretched)	19" (48cm)	20" (51cm)	20½" (52cm)	21" (53.5cm)	23" (58.5cm)
FINISHED HIP	21" (53.5cm)	22" (56cm)	23" (58.5cm)	24" (61cm)	26" (66cm)
FINISHED LENGTH	15" (38cm)	17" (43cm)	19" (48.5cm)	22" (56cm)	24" (61cm)
YARN NEEDED	450 yd (411m)	500 yd (457m)	600 yd (549m)	700 yd (640m)	850 yd (763m)

MATERIALS
450 (500, 600, 700, 850) yards (411 [457, 549, 640, 777]m) of DK-weight yarn: 2 (3, 3, 3, 4) skeins Mountain Colors *River Twist*, 100% merino wool, 240 yards (220m), 3½ oz (100g), in Stillwater River ③

Size G-6 (4mm) crochet hook, *or size to obtain gauge*

Yarn needle

1 yard (.9m) elastic, 1" (2.5cm) wide

Sewing needle and thread

GAUGE
16 sts and 19 rows = 4" (10cm) over single crochet.

INSTRUCTIONS
Waistband
Ch 17.

Row 1 (RS) Sc in 2nd ch from hook and each ch across—16 sc.

Rows 2–80 (84, 88, 92, 100) Ch 1, turn, working in the back loops only, sc in each sc across—16 sc. Do not fasten off.

Cut a piece of elastic equal to the finished waist measurement (or your baby's waist measurement) plus 1" (2.5cm) for overlap. Overlap the ends by 1" (2.5cm) and sew them together, being careful not to twist the elastic. Place the elastic over WS of the waistband and fold waistband in half lengthwise, encasing the elastic. Pin the long edges of the waistband together.

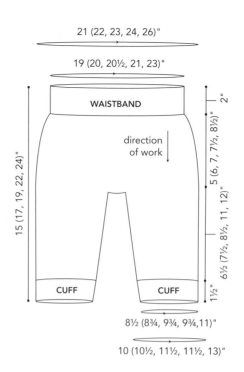

21 (22, 23, 24, 26)"

19 (20, 20½, 21, 23)"

WAISTBAND

direction
of work

15 (17, 19, 22, 24)"

2"

5 (6, 7, 7½, 8½)"

6½ (7½, 8½, 11, 12)"

1½"

CUFF   CUFF

8½ (8¾, 9¾, 9¾, 11)"

10 (10½, 11½, 11½, 13)"

Hips

Round 1 (RS) With RS of waistband facing, working through both layers in ends of rows to encase elastic and removing pins as you go, ch 1, *sc in end of next 19 (20, 21, 22, 24) rows, 2 sc in end of next row; repeat from * 3 more times; join with sl st in first sc—84 (88, 92, 96, 104) sc.

Rounds 2–4 Ch 1, sc in each sc around; join with sl st in first sc.

Round 5 Ch 1, sc in first 44 (46, 48, 50, 54) sts, hdc in next 4 (4, 5, 5, 6) sts, dc in next 30 (32, 32, 34, 36) sts, hdc in next 4 (4, 5, 5, 6) sts, sc in remaining 2 (2, 2, 2, 2) sts, join with sl st in first sc—46 (48, 50, 52, 56) sc, 8 (8, 10, 10, 12) hdc, and 30 (32, 32, 34, 36) dc.

Rounds 6–8 Repeat Round 2.

Rounds 9–24 (28, 32, 36, 40) Repeat Rounds 5–8, 4 (5, 6, 7, 8) times.

NOTE: *For a longer or shorter rise, add or subtract repeats of Rounds 5–8 here. If the baby you are making these for is present, try the pants on before you continue to the legs to ensure a proper fit.*

Size 6–12 months (12–18 months) only
Round 29 (33) Repeat Round 2.

Fasten off.

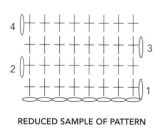

REDUCED SAMPLE OF PATTERN

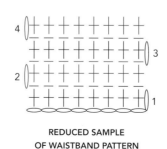

**REDUCED SAMPLE
OF WAISTBAND PATTERN**

STITCH KEY

⬭ = chain (ch)

+ = single crochet (sc)

— = worked in back loop only

Gusset

Skip first 17 (18, 19, 19, 21) sts of round; join yarn in next st.

Row 1 Ch 1, sc in same st as join, sc in next 7 (7, 7, 9, 9) sts.

Rows 2–6 (6, 8, 8, 10) Ch 1, turn, sc in each sc across.

Fasten off. Sew last row of the gusset to opposite side of back of pants, making sure leg openings are equal. Each leg opening should have 34 (36, 38, 38, 42) unworked sts.

Legs

With RS facing, join yarn in leg opening at inseam (inside edge of leg opening).

Round 1 Work 40 (42, 46, 46, 52) sc evenly spaced around leg opening—40 (42, 46, 46, 52) sc.

Round 2 Ch 1, sc in each sc around; join with sl st in first sc.

Repeat Round 2 until leg measures 6½ (7½, 8½, 11, 12)" (16.5 [19, 21.5, 28, 30.5]cm) or 1½" (3.8cm) less than desired leg length. Fasten off.

Repeat for second leg.

> **TIP** There are so many ways to change the look of these pants. Try using a second color for the waistband and the cuffs to make the ribbed texture stand out, or switch between two colors every few rows for a stripy look. Play with the length of the legs and substitute any edging for the cuff, and you'll be able to create soakers, shorts, capris, and pants for your baby—all from one pattern!

Cuff (make 2)

Ch 7.

Row 1 (RS) Sc in 2nd ch from hook and each ch across— 6 sc.

Row 2–40 (42, 46, 46, 52) Ch 1, turn, working in back loops only, sc in each sc across.

Fasten off.

Finishing

With right sides together, align one long edge of a cuff with a leg opening. Whipstitch the lengthwise edge of the cuff to the bottom of the leg, then whipstitch the short ends of the cuff together. Repeat for the second cuff.

Sew the open edge of the waistband shut.

Weave in all ends.

TRY THIS!

Substitute Mountain Colors *River Twist* in Firehole River.

swing set cardigan

This roomy sweater is the perfect outer layer for children on the move. Because it is crocheted from the top down, you can try it on your little one as you work—plus there are no seams to sew at the end! I chose three vintage buttons from my grandmother's collection for this sweater; add your own heirloom buttons or embellishment for a personal touch.

SKILL LEVEL
Easy

SIZES	0–9 months	9–18 months	18–30 months	3–4 years
FINISHED CHEST	21½" (55cm)	24" (61cm)	26" (66cm)	28" (71cm)
FINISHED LENGTH	10" (25.5cm)	11" (28cm)	12½" (32cm)	13¾" (35cm)
YARN NEEDED	350 yd (320m)	375 yd (343m)	400 yd (366m)	475 yd (434m)

MATERIALS
350 (375, 400, 475) yards (320 [343, 366, 434]m) of DK-weight yarn: Shown in: 2 (2, 2, 2) skeins Caron International *Spa*, 75% microdenier acrylic, 25% rayon from bamboo, 251 yards (230m), 3 oz (85g), #0006 Berry Frappe **(3)**

Size F-5 (3.75mm) crochet hook, *or size to obtain gauge*

Yarn needle

3 buttons, ½" (13mm) diameter

Sewing needle

GAUGE
18 sts and 14 rows = 4" (10cm) over hdc;

4 shells = 4⅜" (11cm) and 8 rows = 4" (10cm) over shell pattern.

PATTERN STITCH
Shell Pattern: Worked over a multiple of 6 sts + 1.

Row 1 Ch 3, turn, *sk next 2 dc, (2 dc, ch 1, 2 dc) in next ch-1 sp, sk next 2 dc, dc in next dc; repeat from * across.

Repeat Row 1 for shell pattern.

INSTRUCTIONS
NOTE: *The cardigan is worked from the top down. The yoke is worked first in half double crochet, then in the shell pattern. The piece is then divided for the body and two armholes. The body is worked in the shell pattern from the armholes down to the hem. The sleeve edging is added after the body is complete.*

Yoke
Ch 51 (61, 71, 81).

Row 1 Hdc in 3rd ch from hook (beginning ch counts as first hdc) and in each ch across—50 (60, 70, 80) hdc.

NOTE: *Row 1 is the RS for sizes 0–9 months and 9–18 months, but it is the WS for sizes 18–24 months and 3–4 years.*

Row 2 Ch 2 (counts as first hdc here and throughout), turn, hdc in next 3 (4, 5, 6) hdc, 2 hdc in next hdc, [hdc in next 4 (5, 6, 7) hdc, 2 hdc in next hdc] 9 times—60 (70, 80, 90) hdc.

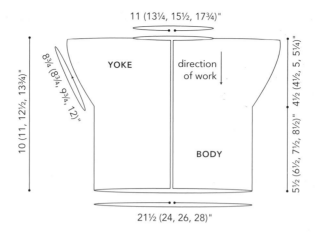

11 (13¼, 15½, 17¾)"

YOKE

direction of work

8¾ (8¾, 9¾, 12)"

10 (11, 12½, 13¾)"

BODY

4½ (4½, 5, 5¼)"

5½ (6½, 7½, 8½)"

21½ (24, 26, 28)"

Row 3 Ch 2, turn, hdc in next 4 (5, 6, 7) hdc, 2 hdc in next hdc, [hdc in next 5 (6, 7, 8) hdc, 2 hdc in next hdc] 9 times—70 (80, 90, 100) hdc.

Row 4 Ch 2, turn, hdc in next 5 (6, 7, 8) hdc, 2 hdc in next hdc, [hdc in next 6 (7, 8, 9) hdc, 2 hdc in next hdc] 9 times—80 (90, 100, 110) hdc.

Row 5 Ch 2, turn, hdc in next 6 (7, 8, 9) hdc, 2 hdc in next hdc, [hdc in next 7 (8, 9, 10) hdc, 2 hdc in next hdc] 9 times—90 (100, 110, 120) hdc.

Row 6 Ch 2, turn, hdc in next 7 (8, 9, 10) hdc, 2 hdc in next hdc, [hdc in next 8 (9, 10, 11) hdc, 2 hdc in next hdc] 9 times—100 (110, 120, 130) hdc.

Row 7 Ch 2, turn, hdc in next 8 (9, 10, 11) hdc, 2 hdc in next hdc, [hdc in next 9 (10, 11, 12) hdc, 2 hdc in next hdc] 9 times—110 (120, 130, 140) hdc.

Row 8 Ch 2, turn, hdc in next 9 (10, 11, 12) hdc, 2 hdc in next hdc, [hdc in next 10 (11, 12, 13) hdc, 2 hdc in next hdc] 9 times—120 (130, 140, 150) hdc.

Row 9 Ch 2, turn, hdc in next 10 (11, 12, 13) hdc, 2 hdc in next hdc, *hdc in next 11 (12, 13, 14) hdc, 2 hdc in next hdc; repeat from * across, work hdc in any remaining sts—130 (140, 150, 160) hdc.

Row 10 Ch 2, turn, hdc in next 16 (26, 11, 14) hdc, 2 hdc in next hdc, *hdc in next 17 (27, 12, 15) hdc, 2 hdc in next hdc; repeat from * across to last 4 (0, 7, 0) hdc, hdc in last 4 (0, 7, 0) hdc—137 (145, 161, 170) hdc.

Size 18–30 months only
Row 11 Ch 2, turn, hdc in each hdc across.

Size 3–4 years only
Row 11 Ch 2, turn, hdc in next 15 hdc, 2 hdc in next hdc, *hdc in next 16 hdc, 2 hdc in next hdc; repeat from * across—180 hdc.

Row 12 Ch 2, turn, hdc in next 34 hdc, 2 hdc in next hdc, *hdc in next 35 hdc, 2 hdc in next hdc; repeat from * across—185 hdc.

BEGIN SHELL PATTERN (all sizes)
Row 11 (11, 12, 13) Ch 1, turn, sc in first hdc, *sk next hdc, (2 dc, ch 1, 2 dc) in next hdc (shell made), sk next hdc, sc in next hdc; repeat from * across—34 (36, 40, 46) shells, 35 (37, 41, 47) sc.

Row 12 (12, 13, 14) Ch 3 (counts as dc here and throughout), turn, *sk next 2 dc, (2 dc, ch 1, 2 dc) in next ch-1 sp, sk next 2 dc, dc in next sc; repeat from * across.

Row 13 (13, 14, 15) Ch 3, turn, *sk next 2 dc, (2 dc, ch 1, 2 dc) in next ch-1 sp, sk next 2 dc, dc in next dc; repeat from * across.

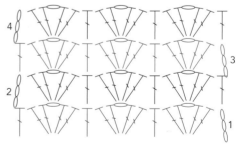

REDUCED SAMPLE OF SHELL PATTERN

STITCH KEY

= chain (ch)

= double crochet (dc)

DIVIDE FOR SLEEVES

Row 14 (14, 15, 16) Ch 3, turn, [sk next 2 dc, (2 dc, ch 1, 2 dc) in next ch-1 sp, sk next 2 dc, dc in next dc] 4 (5, 5, 6) times, (2 dc, ch 1, 2 dc) in next ch-1 sp, sk next 3 dc, sk next 7 (7, 8, 10) shells (sleeve opening made), dc in next dc, [sk next 2 dc, (2 dc, ch 1, 2 dc) in next ch-1 sp, sk next 2 dc, dc in next dc] 9 (11, 11, 11) times, (2 dc, ch 1, 2 dc) in next ch-1 sp, sk next 3 dc, sk next 7 (7, 8, 10) shells, dc in next dc, [sk next 2 dc, (2 dc, ch 1, 2 dc) in next ch-1 sp, sk next 2 dc, dc in next dc] 5 (6, 6, 7) times—20 (22, 24, 26) shells.

Body

NOTE: *Continue to work in the established pattern around the body of the sweater as directed below; you'll come back to the sleeves later.*

Rows 15 (15, 16, 17)–24 (26, 29, 33) Ch 3, turn, *sk next 2 dc, (2 dc, ch 1, 2 dc) in next ch-1 sp, sk next 2 dc, dc in next dc; repeat from * across.

Row 25 (27, 30, 34) (RS) Ch 1, turn, sc in first dc, *sk next 2 dc, 5 dc in next ch-1 sp, sk next 2 dc, dc in next dc; repeat from * across.

Fasten off.

RIGHT FRONT EDGE/BUTTON BAND

With WS facing, join yarn in top right corner of cardigan.

Row 1 Ch 1, sc evenly across right front edge to the lower front corner.

NOTE: *Ensure that you have at least 13 (13, 16, 16) sc across the hdc portion of the cardigan.*

Row 2 Ch 1, turn, sc in each sc to the hdc portion of the cardigan, [sc in next 2 (2, 3, 3) sc, ch 2, sk next 2 sc] 3 times (3 buttonholes made), sc in remaining sc across.

Row 3 Ch 1, turn, sl st in each sc and ch across.

Fasten off.

LEFT FRONT EDGE

With RS facing, join yarn in top left corner of cardigan.

Row 1 Work as for Row 1 of Right Front.

Row 2 Work as for Row 3 of Right Front.

Fasten off.

Sleeves

NOTE: *Sleeves are worked in rounds in the skipped shells of the armhole.*

Round 1 With RS facing, join yarn in ch-1 sp of last skipped shell before underarm, ch 3, 4 dc in same ch-1 sp, work (sc, 5 dc) over underarm sp, *sc in next dc, sk next 2 dc, 5 dc in next ch-1 sp, sk next 2 dc; repeat from * around, sc in last dc; join with sl st in top of beginning ch—8 (8, 9, 11) shells.

Repeat for other sleeve.

Finishing

With a sewing needle and a strand of working yarn, sew 3 buttons to the Right Front of the cardigan, directly across from the buttonholes. Weave in all ends.

> **TIP** Adapt the size and color palette of this sweet sweater without a fuss. For a multicolor cardigan, work the yoke in one color, then change colors every row when you get to the shell pattern. Add or subtract shell rows to easily modify the length of both the sleeves and the body of the sweater to custom-fit the pattern for any child.

tiny tee appliqués

There's nothing cuter than tiny T-shirts, except for those you embellish with your own creative crochet touches. These sweet appliqués work up quickly with just a few skeins of embroidery floss, or hook the patterns with heavier yarn to make larger patches. Use the appliqués to accent basic clothing, or sew them over stains or rips to rejuvenate hand-me-downs.

SKILL LEVEL
Intermediate

SIZE	one size
FINISHED ROCKET (not including wings)	1¾" (4.5cm) wide x 3" (7.5cm) long
FINISHED FLAME	2" (5cm) wide x 1¾" (4.5cm) long
FINISHED LARGE FLOWER	1½" (3.8cm) in diameter
FINISHED SMALL FLOWER	1" (2.5cm) in diameter
FINISHED SMALL CIRCLE	⅝" (16mm) in diameter
YARN NEEDED	8¾ yards (8m) each of five colors per project

MATERIALS
43½ yards (40m) of fingering weight yarn: DMC 6-Strand Embroidery Floss, 100% cotton, 8¾ yards (8m) as follows for each set of appliqués.

Rocket Shirt (opposite): 1 skein each in #995 blue (A), #321 red (B), #727 yellow (C), #314 light orange (D), and #720 orange (E) 🅘

Floral Shirt and Shorts Set (page 100): 1 skein each in #727 yellow (F), #720 orange (G), #3608 light pink (H), #3607 dark pink (I), and #550 purple (J) 🅘

Size C-2 (2.75mm) crochet hook, *or size to obtain gauge*

Yarn needle

Sewing needle

Three star-shaped buttons, ⅝" (16mm) diameter (optional)

Two star-shaped buttons, ½" (13mm) diameter (optional)

GAUGE
Gauge is not critical for this project. Refer to finished measurements for each motif to check your gauge—each motif works up almost as quickly as a gauge swatch.

INSTRUCTIONS
Rocket Appliqué
With A, ch 17.

Row 1 (RS) Dc in 4th ch from hook (beginning ch counts as dc), dc in next 12 ch, (3 dc, ch 1, 3 dc) in next ch; rotate piece to work across opposite side of foundation ch, dc in each remaining ch across and in bottom of beginning ch—34 dc (17 dc along each side, with a ch-1 sp at tip).

Row 2 Ch 3, turn, dc in next 13 dc, 2 dc in next 2 dc, (dc, tr) in next dc, ch 1, sk next ch-1 sp, (tr, dc) in next dc, 2 dc in next 2 dc, dc in remaining 14 dc—38 dc, 2 tr, and 1 ch-1 sp at tip.

Round 3 Ch 3, turn, dc in next 8 dc, hdc in next 5 dc, (hdc, sc) in next dc, sc in next 5 sts, (sc, ch 1, sc) in next ch-1 sp, sc in next 5 sts, (sc, hdc) in next dc, hdc in next 5 dc, dc in next 9 dc, ch 1; rotate piece to work in ends of rows, work 12 sc evenly spaced across lower edge of rocket; join with sl st in first dc—18 dc, 12 hdc, and 26 sc.

Fasten off.

MAKE FIRST WING

NOTE: *Wings are worked directly onto rocket piece. With RS of rocket facing, join B in one lower corner of rocket.*

Row 1 (RS) Ch 3, working in back loops only, dc in same st as join, 2 dc in next dc, dc in next 7 dc, hdc in next st, (sc, sl st) in next st; leave remaining sts unworked—11 dc, 1 hdc, and 1 sc.

Row 2 Ch 1, turn, sc in first sc, hdc in next 2 sts, dc in next 7 dc, 2 dc in last 3 sts, ch 1; working in ends of rows, work 2 sc in end of each dc row, sl st in same st as first st of Row 1—5 sc, 2 hdc, and 13 dc.

Row 3 Ch 1, turn, sl st in each st across bottom and side of wing. Fasten off.

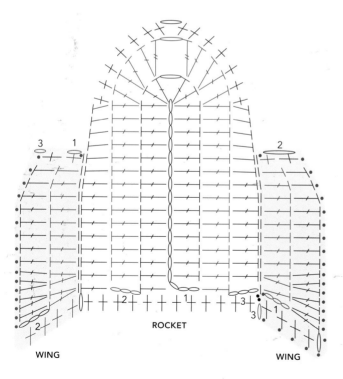

ROCKET

WING

WING

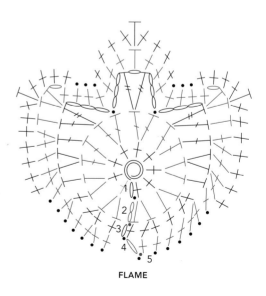

FLAME

MAKE SECOND WING

With RS of rocket facing, count 10 sts from remaining lower corner of rocket and join B in next st (the 11th st from lower edge), to work back down toward lower edge.

Row 1 (RS) Working in back loops only, ch 1, sc in same st as join, hdc in next st, dc in next 7 sts, 2 dc in next 2 dc—1 sc, 1 hdc, and 11 dc.

Row 2 Ch 3, turn, dc in first st, 2 dc in next 2 dc, dc in next 7 dc, hdc in next 2 sts, sc in sc—13 dc, 2 hdc, and 1 sc.

Row 3 Ch 1, turn, sl st across wing; working in ends of rows, work 2 sc in end of each dc row—4 sc. Fasten off.

FLAME

With C, make an adjustable ring.

Round 1 (RS) Ch 1, 9 sc in ring; join with sl st in first sc—9 sc.

Round 2 Ch 2 (does not count as a st), 2 hdc in next 3 sc, 2 dc in next 4 sc, 2 hdc in last 2 sc; join with sl st in first hdc—10 hdc and 8 dc.

Round 3 Ch 1, [sc in next hdc, 2 sc in next hdc] twice, hdc in next hdc, 2 hdc in next hdc, dc in next dc, (dc, tr) in next dc, ch 3, sl st in next dc, ch 3, (tr, ch 1, tr) in next dc, ch 3, sl st in next dc, ch 3, (tr, dc) in next dc, dc in next dc, 2 hdc in next dc, hdc in next hdc, sc in next hdc, 2 sc in next hdc, sc in last hdc; join with sl st in first sc—10 sc, 6 hdc, 4 dc, 4 tr, 4 ch-3 sps, and 1 ch-1 sp. Fasten off C.

Round 4 Join D in first st, ch 1, sk joining st, sc in next 3 sc, [sc in next st, 2 sc in next st] 3 times, hdc in next dc, (2 hdc, ch 1, sc) in next tr, work 5 sc evenly spaced over next 6 ch (evenly over the 2 ch-3 sps), sc in next tr, hdc in next ch-1 sp, sc in next tr, work 5 sc across next 6 ch, (sc, ch 1, 2 hdc) in next tr, hdc in next dc, [2 sc in next st, sc in next st] 4 times; join with sl st in first sc—38 sc, 7 hdc, and 2 ch-1 sps. Fasten off D.

Round 5 (RS) Join E in first st, sl st in first 6 sts, sc in next 6 sts, (sc, hdc, sc) in next st, sc in next hdc, sc in next ch-1 sp, sc in next sc, sl st in next 3 sc, sc in next 3 sc, (sc, hdc, sc) in hdc, sc in next 3 sc, sl st in next 3 sc, sc in next sc, sc in next ch-1 sp, sc in next hdc, (sc, hdc, sc) in next hdc, sc in next 6 sts, sl st in remaining 7 sts; join with sl st in first sl st. Fasten off. To finish, refer to page 100.

STITCH KEY

⬭ = chain (ch)

• = slip st (sl st)

+ = single crochet (sc)

T = half double crochet (hdc)

丅 = double crochet (dc)

丅 = treble crochet

— = worked in back loop only

◎ = adjustable ring

Floral Appliqués

LARGE FLOWER (make 4)

Work one each in the following color sequences: F/G/I, G/H/J, F/I/H, and H/J/G.

With first color, make an adjustable ring.

Round 1 (RS) Ch 2 (does not count as a stitch), 8 hdc in ring; join with sl st in first hdc—8 hdc. Drop, but do not cut, first color.

Round 2 Join 2nd color in first hdc, ch 1, 2 sc in each hdc around; join with sl st in first sc—16 sc. Fasten off 2nd color.

Round 3 With first color, ch 1, [sc in next sc, 2 sc in next sc] 8 times; join with sl st in first sc—24 sc. Fasten off first color.

Round 4 (RS) Join third color in first st, ch 1, 3 dc in next sc (petal made), [ch 1, sl st in next 2 sc, ch 1, 3 dc in next sc] 7 times, ch 1, sl st in last sc—8 petals.

Fasten off.

SMALL FLOWER (make 2)

Work one each in the following color sequences: G/H and H/J.

Work as for Large Flower through Round 1. Fasten off first color.

Round 2 Join 2nd color in first hdc, (ch 1, 2 dc, ch 1, sl st) in same hdc as join (petal made), (sl st, ch 1, 2 dc, ch 1, sl st) in next 7 hdc; join with sl st in first hdc of round 1—8 petals. Fasten off.

SMALL CIRCLE (make 1)

Work one each in the following sequences: I/J/F and G/F/I.

Work as for Large Flower through Round 2. Fasten off first and 2nd colors.

Round 3 Join third color in first st, sl st in each sc around; join with sl st in first sl st.

Fasten off.

Finishing (all appliqués)

Weave in all ends.

To attach appliqués, thread a needle with 1 strand of embroidery floss in the same color as the final round of the appliqué. Sew the appliqué to the garment, referring to the photograph for placement. To finish the Rocket Shirt, sew five star buttons to the T-shirt, scattered around the appliqué, or embroider stars instead of using buttons.

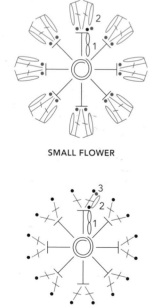

SMALL FLOWER

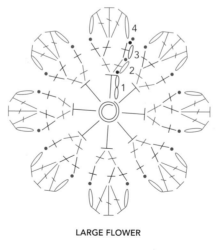

LARGE FLOWER

SMALL CIRCLE

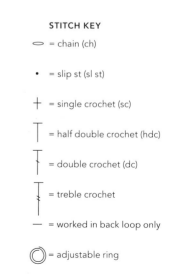

STITCH KEY

◯ = chain (ch)

• = slip st (sl st)

+ = single crochet (sc)

T = half double crochet (hdc)

╪ = double crochet (dc)

= treble crochet

— = worked in back loop only

◎ = adjustable ring

ribbed cardigan

Combine lacy floral motifs with mock ribbing that's worked from side to side to create this cute sweater. Simple changes in stitch height create the gentle flare that gives this garment a swingy, vintage look. The cardigan is worked in flat pieces that are sewn together, making it a good first foray into crocheting garments.

SKILL LEVEL
Intermediate

SIZES	0–6 months	6–12 months	12–18 months
FINISHED CHEST	20" (51cm)	22" (56cm)	24" (61cm)
FINISHED LENGTH	10¾" (27cm)	11" (28cm)	12" (30.5cm)
YARN NEEDED	620 yd (567m)	720 yd (658m)	840 yd (768m)

MATERIALS
620 (720, 840) yards (567 [658, 768]m) of sportweight yarn: 4 (5, 5) skeins Lana Grossa *Cool Wool 2000*, 100% wool, 175 yards (160m), 1¾ oz (50g), #524 Purple 🔲2

Size 7 (4.5mm) crochet hook, *or size to obtain gauge*

Stitch markers

Yarn needle

2 buttons, 1" (25mm) diameter

GAUGE
18 sts = 4" (10cm), and 10½ rows = 4" (10cm) measured across hdc edge, and 7 rows = 4" (10cm) measured across tr edge over body and sleeve pattern;

Floral motif measures 2½ (2¾, 3)" (6.5 [7, 7.5]cm) square.

SPECIAL STITCH
Cluster (Cl): (Yarn over, insert the hook in stitch, yarn over and draw up a loop, yarn over and draw through 2 loops) twice in the same stitch. Yarn over and draw through all 3 loops on hook.

INSTRUCTIONS
NOTE: *The bodice is constructed from floral motifs that are sewn together to form the top portion of the sweater. The sweater body is worked side to side all in one piece, from one front edge to the other front edge. The sweater body forms the bottom half of the sweater.*

Floral Motif (make 10)
Ch 4; join with sl st in first ch to form a ring.

Round 1 (RS) Ch 3 (does not count as a st), dc in ring (beginning ch and first dc count as first Cl), ch 2, [Cl, ch 2] 7 times in ring; sk beginning ch and join with sl st in first dc—8 clusters.

Round 2 Sl st in next ch-2 sp, ch 3 (does not count as a st), (dc, ch 2, cl) in same ch-2 sp (corner made), ch 1, (dc, ch 1, dc) in next ch-2 sp, ch 1, *(Cl, ch 2, Cl) in next ch-2 sp (corner made), ch 1, (dc, ch 1, dc) in next ch-2 sp, ch 1; repeat from * twice more; sk beginning ch and join with sl st in first dc—8 clusters, and 8 dc.

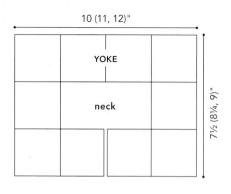

10 (11, 12)"

YOKE

neck

7½ (8¼, 9)"

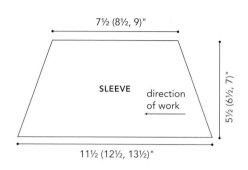

7½ (8½, 9)"

SLEEVE   direction of work ←

5½ (6½, 7)"

11½ (12½, 13½)"

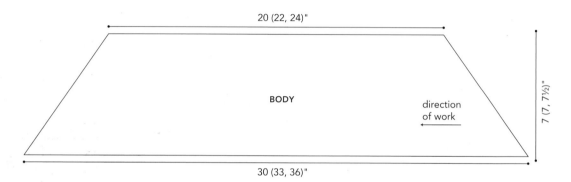

20 (22, 24)"

BODY   direction of work ←

7 (7, 7½)"

30 (33, 36)"

Size 0–6 months only

Round 3 Ch 1, sc in same dc as join, *(2 sc, ch 1, 2 sc) in next corner ch-2 sp, sc in each Cl, ch-1 sp, and dc along side; repeat from * 3 more times; join with sl st in first sc—44 sc.

Size 6–12 months only

Round 3 Ch 2, *(2 hdc, ch 1, 2 hdc) in next corner ch-2 sp, hdc in each Cl, ch-1 sp, and dc along side; repeat from * 3 more times; join with sl st in first hdc—44 hdc.

Size 12–18 months only

Round 3 Ch 3, *(2 dc, ch 1, 2 dc) in next corner ch-2 sp, dc in each Cl, ch-1 sp, and dc along side; repeat from * 3 more times; join with sl st in first dc—44 dc.

Sweater Body (worked in one piece)

Ch 34 (34, 36).

Row 1 (WS) Dc in 4th ch from hook (beginning ch counts as first dc) and each ch across—32 (32, 34) dc.

Row 2 (RS) Ch 2 (counts as hdc here and throughout), turn, working in back loops only, hdc in next 9 (9, 10) sts, dc in next 9 (9, 10) sts, tr in remaining 14 sts—32 (32, 34) sts.

Row 3 Ch 3, turn, working in back loops only, dc in each st across—32 (32, 34) dc.

Rows 4–53 (59, 63) Repeat last 2 rows 25 (28, 30) more times.

Fasten off.

Sleeves (make 2)

Ch 27 (31, 33).

Row 1 (WS) Dc in 4th ch (beginning ch counts as first dc) from hook and each ch across—25 (29, 31) dc.

Row 2 (RS) Ch 2 (counts as hdc here and throughout), turn, working in back loops only, hdc in next 7 (9, 10) sts, dc in next 8 (10, 10) sts, tr in remaining 10 (10, 11) sts—25 (29, 31) sts.

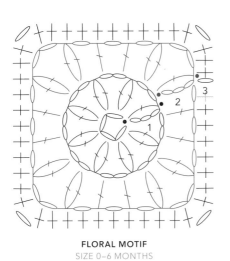

FLORAL MOTIF
SIZE 0–6 MONTHS

FLORAL MOTIF
SIZE 6–12 MONTHS

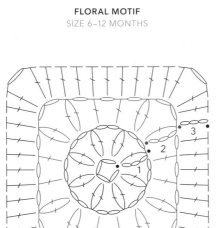

FLORAL MOTIF
SIZE 12–18 MONTHS

STITCH KEY

⬭ = chain (ch)

• = slip st (sl st)

+ = single crochet (sc)

⊤ = half double crochet (hdc)

⊤ = double crochet (dc)

⬮ = cluster (cl)

Row 3 Ch 3, turn, working in the back loops only, dc in each st across—25 (29, 31) dc.

Rows 4–19 (21, 23) Repeat last 2 rows 8 (9, 10) more times.

Row 20 (22, 24) Repeat Row 2.

Fasten off.

Finishing

ASSEMBLY

Sew 10 floral motifs together following the layout shown in the yoke schematic, page 104. With right sides together, align the hdc/dc edge of each sleeve with the edge of the yoke and whipstitch the sleeves in place (Whipstitch Seam, page 152). Fold the yoke in half with the right sides together and whipstitch the sleeve seams. With right sides together, pin the hdc/dc edge of the body piece to the yoke, matching the center of the body with the center back of the bodice and making sure that the front edges of the yoke and body are aligned. Whipstitch the yoke and body together.

EDGING

With RS facing, join yarn with sl st in the lower right front corner to work up front edge.

Round 1 Ch 1, work sc evenly up the front edge to top corner of floral motif, 3 sc in top corner ch-1 sp of floral motif, hdc evenly around the collar to front neck edge, 3 sc in top corner ch-1 sp of floral motif, sc evenly down the left front edge, work 3 sc in lower front corner; working around the posts of the stitches in ends of rows across lower edge, *sc in end of next dc row, work (3 dc, ch 3, 3 dc) in end of next tr row (pointed shell made); repeat from * across lower edge, sc in end of last dc row, work 2 dc in same st as join; join with sl st in first sc—26 (29, 31) pointed shells across lower edge.

Place two markers (for button loops) along front edge of top right floral motif. Place first marker about ½" (1.5cm) below neck edge, and second marker about 2" (5cm) below the first (near lower edge of floral motif).

Round 2 Sl st in each stitch up front edge, around neck, and down opposite front edge, when each button loop marker is reached, work as follows: ch 6 (for button loop), sk next sc, sl st in next sc. Fasten off.

SLEEVE EDGING

With RS facing, and working in ends of rows around lower edge of sleeve, join yarn with sl st in end of any dc row of lower sleeve edge. Work this round of stitches over the posts at the end of the rows, rather than into the stitches themselves, in order to get the lacy effect of the trim.

Round 1 Ch 1, sc in end of same dc row as join, (3 dc, ch 3, 3 dc) in end of next tr row, *sc in end of next dc row, work (3 dc, ch 3, 3 dc) over end of next tr row (pointed shell made); repeat from * around; join with sl st in first sc—10 (11, 12) pointed shells.

Repeat for other sleeve.

HOODED CAPELET

Self-striping sock yarn and a classic ripple stitch pattern turn this simple capelet into something special. It's great for playing dress-up or for warmth when an extra layer of clothing is needed. The cape closes with a button tab for smaller children, or pom-pom neck ties for older ones. For safety reasons, please be sure to supervise your child while he or she is wearing the cape.

SKILL LEVEL

Intermediate

SIZES	6–12 months	12–18 months	2–3 years	4–5 years
FINISHED LENGTH (excluding hood)	12" (30.5cm)	12½" (32cm)	13½" (34.5cm)	15" (38cm)
YARN NEEDED	520 yd (475)	660 yd (604m)	780 yd (713m)	960 yd (878m)

MATERIALS

520 (660, 780, 960) yards (475 [604, 713, 878]m) of sportweight yarn: 2 (3, 3, 4) skeins of Noro *Silk Garden Sock Yarn*, 40% lamb's wool, 25% silk, 25% nylon, 10% kid mohair, 275 yards (300m), 3½ oz (100g), color #S292 pink/purple/gray ❷

Size F-5 (3.75mm) crochet hook, *or size to obtain gauge*

Yarn needle

Stitch markers

Two 1¼" (3cm) diameter buttons or 1½" (3.8cm) diameter pom-pom maker (optional)

GAUGE

18 sts and 9 rows = 4" (10cm) over double crochet.

INSTRUCTIONS

NOTE: *The capelet is worked in one piece. The hood is worked in rows of double crochet down to the neck. The ripple stitch pattern is then established around the neck, and the capelet is worked from the neck down.*

Hood

Ch 62 (72, 82, 92).

Row 1 (RS) Dc in 4th ch from hook (beginning ch counts as first dc) and in each ch across—60 (70, 80, 90) dc.

Rows 2–15 (17, 19, 22) Ch 3 (counts as dc here and throughout), turn, dc in each dc across.

Row 16 (18, 20, 23) Ch 1, turn, sc in each dc across.

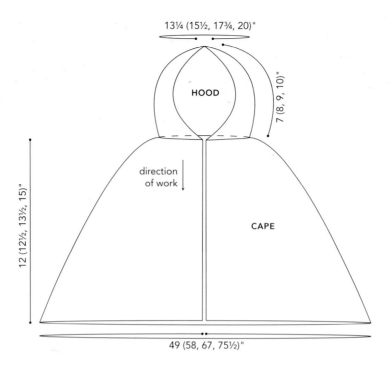

13¼ (15½, 17¾, 20)"

HOOD

7 (8, 9, 10)"

direction of work

CAPE

12 (12½, 13½, 15)"

49 (58, 67, 75½)"

Shape Neck

Row 1 (eyelet row) Ch 1, turn, *sc in next sc, ch 4, sk next 3 sc, sc in next sc; repeat from * across—12 (14, 16, 18) ch-4 sps.

Row 2 Ch 3 (counts as dc here and throughout), turn, dc in first st, 2 dc in next ch-4 sp, (3 dc, ch 2, 3 dc) in each ch-4 sp across to last ch-4 sp, 2 dc in last ch-4 sp, 2 dc in last sc—10 (12, 14, 16) ch-2 sps and 68 (80, 92, 104) dc.

Row 3 Ch 3, turn, dc in first st, dc in next 2 dc, sk next 2 dc, place a marker between last dc made and next dc, *dc in next 2 dc, (2 dc, ch 2, 2 dc) in next ch-2 sp, dc in next 2 dc, sk next 2 dc, place a marker between last dc made and next dc; repeat from * across to last 3 dc, dc in next 2 dc, 2 dc in last dc—88 (104, 120, 136) dc.

Move markers up as work progresses.

Row 4 Ch 3, turn, dc in first st, 2 dc in next dc, dc in each dc to one st before marker, sk next 2 dc, *dc in each dc to next ch-2 sp, (2 dc, ch 2, 2 dc) in next ch-2 sp, dc in each dc to one st before marker, sk next 2 dc; repeat from * across to one st before last marker, sk next 2 dc, dc in each dc to last 2 dc, 2 dc in last 2 dc—110 (130, 150, 170) dc.

Row 5 Ch 3, turn, dc in first st, dc in each dc to one st before marker, *sk next 2 dc, dc in each dc to next ch-2 sp, (dc, ch 2, dc) in next ch-2 sp, dc in each dc to one st before next marker; repeat from * across to one st before last marker, sk next 2 dc, dc in each dc to last dc, 2 dc in last dc.

Row 6 Repeat Row 4—132 (156, 180, 204) dc.

Rows 7 and 8 Repeat Rows 5 and 6—154 (182, 210, 238) dc.

Rows 9–11 Repeat Row 5 three times.

Row 12 Repeat Row 4—176 (208, 240, 272) dc.

Rows 13–20 Repeat Rows 9–12 twice—220 (260, 300, 340) dc.

Row 21–23 (24, 26, 28) Repeat Row 5, 3 (4, 5, 6) times, or to desired length.

Fasten off.

Finishing

Fold the top edge of the hood in half and sew the edges together to form the top of the hood.

EDGING

Round 1 With right side facing, join yarn in lower front corner, ch 1, 2 sc in corner, work 2 sc in end of each row up front edge, around hood edges, and down opposite front edge to opposite lower front corner; work 3 sc in opposite corner, sc in next 9 dc, sc2tog, *sc in next 9 dc, 4 sc in next ch-4 sp, sc in next 9 dc, sc2tog; repeat from * across to last 9 sts, sc in next 9 dc, 2 sc in last dc; join with sl st in first sc.

Row 2 Ch 1, sc in each sc up front edge, around hood edges, and down opposite front edge. Fasten off.

NECK CLOSURE

NOTE: *Both neck ties and buttons can be hazardous for small children. At your discretion, use the Button Tab closure for children under age three, and the Neck Tie closure for older children.*

BUTTON TAB (optional)

Ch 24.

Row 1 Dc in 10th ch from hook (skipped 10 ch forms buttonhole), dc in next 13 ch—14 dc.

Round 2 Ch 1, turn, evenly sc around entire outside edge of tab, working 14 sc into ch-10 sp.

Fasten off. Pin the non-loop edge of the tab to the Right Front of the cape just below the hood. Place one button over the tab, and sew both the button and tab to the cardigan. Sew the remaining button to the Left Front, directly across from button loop.

NECK TIE (for kids ages 3 and up, optional)

With 2 strands of yarn held together, work a chain that is 32" (81.5cm) in length. Fasten off. Weave the chain through the eyelet row at the neck of cape. Following the manufacturer's instructions, make two 1½"- (3.8cm-) diameter pom-poms. Sew one pom-pom to each end of the tie.

Weave in all ends.

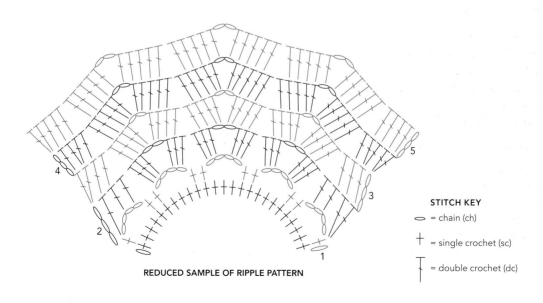

REDUCED SAMPLE OF RIPPLE PATTERN

STITCH KEY

⬯ = chain (ch)

✝ = single crochet (sc)

⊤ = double crochet (dc)

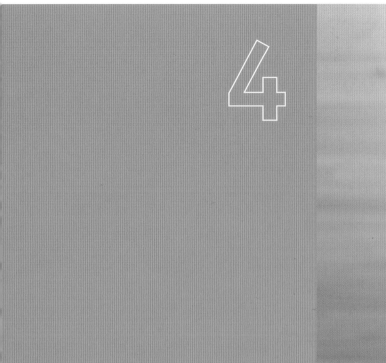

4

LITTLE
GIFTS

star Booties

These simple booties work up quickly with just a tiny bit of yarn. There's no fancy stitch work required, and you can complete them in just a few hours. Whether you pair them with a Beanie or Bonnet (page 120) or wrap them up to give all on their own, these booties are sure to be an "aww!"-inspiring gift at baby showers.

SKILL LEVEL
Easy

SIZES	0–3 months	3–6 months
FINISHED LENGTH OF SOLE	3½" (9cm)	3¾" (9.5cm)
COLOR A	40 yd (37m)	50 yd (46m)
COLOR B	10 yd (9m)	10 yd (9m)

MATERIALS
50 (60) yd (46 [55]m) of worsted-weight yarn: Noro *Cash Iroha*, 40% silk, 30% lamb's wool, 20% cashmere, 10% nylon, 31.4 oz (40g), 99 yd (91m) (④)

Booties A (left): 1 skein each #109 Lime Green (A) and #125 Cranberry (B)

Booties B (right): 1 skein each #108 Brown (A) and #109 Lime Green (B)

Size G-6 (4mm) crochet hook, *or size to obtain gauge*

Yarn needle

1 yd (.9m) elastic sewing thread (optional)

GAUGE
Gauge is not critical for this project.

INSTRUCTIONS
NOTE: *First, the sole is worked in rounds. Then the sides and heel of the bootie are worked in rows across three sides of the sole. The remaining stitches at the toe are left unworked. The upper is made separately and sewn to the toe opening.*

Sole (make 2)

With A, ch 11.

Round 1 (RS) 5 dc in 4th ch from hook (beginning ch counts as dc), dc in next 4 ch, hdc in next 2 ch, 4 hdc in next ch; rotate piece to work across opposite side of foundation ch, hdc in next 2 ch, dc in next 4 ch; join with sl st in top of beginning ch—8 hdc and 14 dc.

Round 2 Ch 3 (counts as dc here and throughout), dc in first st, 2 dc in next 5 dc, dc in next 6 sts, 2 dc in next 4 hdc, dc in last 6 sts; join with sl st in top of beginning ch—32 dc.

Size 0–3 months only

Round 3 Ch 1, working in the back loops only, sc in each st around; join with sl st in first sc—32 sc.

NOTE: *Work now progresses in back and forth in rows to form the sides and heel of the bootie. Leave the other stitches unworked, for the toe of the bootie.*

Row 4 Ch 1, turn, sc2tog, sc in next 16 sc, sc2tog, leave remaining sts unworked—18 sc.

Row 5 Ch 1, turn, sc2tog, sc in next 14 sc, sc2tog—16 sc.

Row 6 Ch 1, turn, sc in next 16 sc—16 sc.

Round 7 Ch 1, turn, sc in next 16 sc, ch 4 (for front of ankle); join with sl st in first sc of round.

Fasten off.

Size 3–6 months only

Round 3 Ch 1, [sc in first 2 dc, 2 sc in next dc] 4 times, sc in next 9 dc, 2 sc in next 2 dc, sc in remaining 9 dc; join with sl st in first sc—38 sc.

Rounds 4 and 5 Ch 1, working in the back loops only, sc in each sc around; join with sl st in first sc.

NOTE: *Work now progresses back and forth in rows to form the sides and heel of the bootie. Leave the other stitches unworked, for the toe of the bootie.*

Row 6 Ch 1, turn, sc2tog, sc in next 19 sc, sc2tog; leave remaining sts unworked—21 sc.

Row 7 Ch 1, turn, sc2tog, sc in next 17 sc, sc2tog, sc in next unworked st of previous row—19 sc.

Row 8 Ch 1, turn, sc in each sc across—19 sc.

Round 9 Turn, sl st in each sc across, ch 4 (for front of ankle); join with sl st in first sl st of round.

Fasten off.

Upper Motif (make 2)

Make an adjustable ring.

Round 1 (RS) With B, ch 3 (counts as hdc, ch 1), [hdc in ring, ch 1] 5 times; join with sl st in 2nd ch of beginning ch—6 hdc and 6 ch-1 sps. Fasten off.

Round 2 Join A in any ch-1 sp, ch 3, 2 dc in same ch-1 sp as join, 3 dc in each ch-1 sp around, join with sl st in top of beginning ch—18 dc.

Fasten off, leaving a 10" (25.5cm) long tail for sewing.

Finishing

Place the Upper Motif over the Sole of the bootie. Using the long tail, whipstitch the motif to the toe of the bootie. Weave in all ends.

TIP To make sure these booties fit snugly, thread a piece of elastic sewing thread through the inside of the last round of stitches at the ankle. Tie the thread off to a length slightly shorter than the opening of the bootie and weave in all ends.

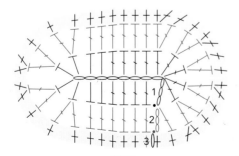

SOLE
NOTE: *Round 3 (shaded aread) is for Size 3–6 Months only*

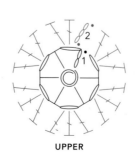

UPPER

STITCH KEY

⌒ = chain (ch)

• = slip st (sl st)

+ = single crochet (sc)

T = half double crochet (hdc)

⊤ = double crochet (dc)

◎ = adjustable ring

NO FUSS PARTY BIBS

Dress up your baby for any occasion with these sweet and simple bibs. A bow tie for him and ruffles for her lend a festive look that's also perfect for everyday use. It's almost unbelievable how many bibs a baby goes through in a day, but this simple pattern makes it easy to stitch up several before the baby arrives. An adjustable neck strap means parents can continue to use these bibs as their baby grows; crochet them in washable cotton for easy care and durability.

SKILL LEVEL
Easy

SIZE	one size
FINISHED MEASUREMENTS (in diameter, excluding strap and ruffle)	7½" (19cm)
YARN NEEDED	120 yd (110m)

MATERIALS
120 yards (110m) (per bib) of worsted-weight yarn:
Coats and Clark *Crème de la Crème*, 100% combed cotton, 126 yards (115m), 2½ oz (71g) (**4**)

Ruffle Bib (opposite): 1 skein each #0910 Wood Violet (A)

Bow Tie Bib (page 118): 1 skein each #0118 Linen (B) and #0984 Blue Tones (C)

Size F-5 (3.75mm) crochet hook, *or size to obtain gauge*

Yarn needle

2 buttons per bib, ½–¾" (13–19mm) diameter

Sewing needle and thread

GAUGE
Rounds 1–5 = 4½" (11.5cm) diameter.

INSTRUCTIONS
Bib

With A (Ruffle Bib) or B (Bow Tie Bib), make an adjustable ring.

Round 1 (RS) Ch 3 (counts as first dc here and throughout), 9 dc in ring; join with sl st in top of beginning ch—10 dc.

Round 2 Ch 3, dc in same st as join, 2 dc in each dc around; join with sl st in top of beginning ch—20 dc.

Round 3 Ch 3, 2 dc in next dc, [dc in next dc, 2 dc in next dc] 9 times; join with sl st in top of beginning ch—30 dc.

Round 4 Ch 3, dc in next dc, 2 dc in next dc, [dc in next 2 dc, 2 dc in next dc] 9 times; join with sl st in top of beginning ch—40 dc.

Round 5 Ch 3, dc in next 2 dc, 2 dc in next dc, [dc in next 3 dc, 2 dc in next dc] 9 times; join with sl st in top of beginning ch—50 dc.

STITCH KEY

⬯ = chain (ch)

• = slip st (sl st)

+ = single crochet (sc)

┬ = double crochet (dc)

⋀ = single crochet 2 together (sc2tog)

STRAP

RUFFLE

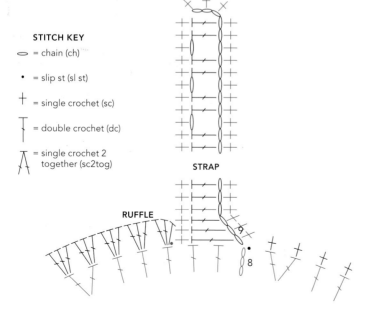

9

• 8

BOW

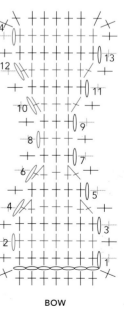

14

12

10

8

6

4

2

13

11

9

7

5

3

1

Round 6 Ch 3, dc in next 3 dc, 2 dc in next dc, [dc in next 4 dc, 2 dc in next dc] 9 times; join with sl st in top of beginning ch—60 dc.

Round 7 Ch 3, dc in next 4 dc, 2 dc in next dc, [dc in next 5 dc, 2 dc in next dc] 9 times; join with sl st in top of beginning ch—70 dc.

Round 8 Ch 3, dc in next 5 dc, 2 dc in next dc, [dc in next 6 dc, 2 dc in next dc] 9 times; join with sl st in top of beginning ch—80 dc.

Do not fasten off. Proceed with Ruffle Bib or Bow Tie Bib Edge.

Ruffle Bib Edge

Round 9 Ch 48 (to begin strap), dc in 4th ch from hook, dc in next ch, [ch 1, sk next dc, dc in next 2 dc] 3 times (3 buttonholes made), dc in each remaining ch, sk next 2 dc of bib, (sl st, hdc, 2 dc) in next dc, 3 dc in next 62 dc, (2 dc, hdc) in next dc, sc in remaining sts of bib; working across opposite side of strap foundation ch, sc in each ch across, sc in each ch at beginning of strap, sc in each dc and ch-1 sp across other side of strap. Fasten off.

Bow Tie Bib Edge

Round 9 Ch 48 (to begin strap), dc in 4th ch from hook, dc in next ch, [ch 1, sk next dc, dc in next 2 dc] 3 times (3 buttonholes made), dc in each remaining ch, sk next 2 dc of bib, (sl st, ch 1, sc) in next dc, sc in next 6 dc, 2 dc in next dc, [sc in next 7 dc, 2 sc in next dc] 7 times, 2 sc in next dc, sc in remaining sts of bib; working across opposite side of strap foundation ch, sc in each ch across, sc in each ch at beginning of strap, sc in each dc and ch-1 sp across other side of strap. Fasten off.

Bow

With C, ch 8.

Row 1 (RS) Sc in 2nd ch from hook and in each remaining ch across—7 sc.

Rows 2 and 3 Ch 1, turn, sc in each sc across.

Row 4 Ch 1, turn, sc2tog, sc in each sc to last 2 sc, sc2tog—5 sc.

Rows 5 and 6 Repeat Rows 3 and 4—3 sc.

Rows 7–9 Repeat Row 2.

Row 10 Ch 1, turn, 2 sc in first sc, sc in each sc to last sc, 2 sc in last sc—5 sc.

Rows 11 and 12 Repeat Rows 9 and 10—7 sc.

Rows 13 and 14 Repeat Row 2.

Round 15 Ch 1, turn, sc evenly around outside edge of bow, working 2 sc in each corner.

Fasten off.

CENTER BAND

With C, ch 9.

Row 1 (RS) Sc in 2nd ch from hook and in each remaining ch across—8 sc.

Row 2 Ch 1, turn, sc in each sc across.

Fasten off, leaving a long tail. Wrap Band around center of Bow and sew the short sides of the Band together on the back side of the Bow. Sew the Bow to the Bib.

Finishing

Weave in all ends. Sew a button to both sides of the top of the Bow Tie Bib. One button is used to secure the strap, the other is for decoration.

TIP You can also use the crochet bow included in this pattern to make hair clips. Try a lightweight yarn and a smaller hook for a pair that's perfectly sized for kids.

beanie and bonnet

Hats are one of the most frequently made gifts for kids—they're simple, cute, and use very little yarn. But when it comes to little ones, keeping a hat on a child's head can be a bit of a challenge! To that end, I've written this pattern in two ways: as a beanie and a modern bonnet. The bonnet includes a chin strap that both secures the hat and highlights chubby baby cheeks in an adorable way. Both styles sport a fun zig-zag border and are sized for kids of all ages. Be sure to compare your child's head measurement to the finished measurements to determine which size to crochet.

SKILL LEVEL
Intermediate

SIZES	baby	toddler	child
FINISHED CIRCUMFERENCE (unstretched)	14" (35.5cm)	16½" (42cm)	19" (48.5cm)
COLOR A	65 yd (60m)	75 yd (69m)	90 yd (83m)
COLORS B AND C	30 yd (28m) each	35 yd (32m) each	45 yd (41m) each

NOTE: *To use just two colors, as in the beanie, double the amount needed for the stripe color.*

MATERIALS
125 (145, 180) yards (115 [133, 165]m) of worsted-weight yarn: 1 skein each of Noro *Cash Iroha*, 40% silk, 30% lamb's wool, 20% cashmere, 10% nylon, 99 yards (91m), 31.4 oz (40g) (4)

Beanie (page 123): #109 Lime Green (A) and #120 Medium Grey (B)

Bonnet (opposite): #120 Medium Grey (A), #125 Cranberry (B), and #109 Pale Pink (C)

Size E-4 (3.5mm) crochet hook, *or size to obtain gauge*

Yarn needle

One heart-shaped button, 1½" (3.8cm) diameter (for Bonnet)

GAUGE
Rounds 1–4 = 3½" (9cm) diameter.

SPECIAL STITCH
V-Stitch Decrease (V-st dec): Yarn over and insert hook in same st as for stitch just made, yarn over and draw up a loop (3 loops on hook, first leg of V-st made), sk next st, yarn over and insert hook in next st, yarn over and draw up a loop (2nd leg of V-st made), yarn over and draw through all 5 loops on hook.

NOTE: *When the stitch just made was a V-st, insert hook in same st as 2nd leg of the prior V-st.*

INSTRUCTIONS

Beanie

With A, make an adjustable ring.

Round 1 (RS) Ch 3 (counts as dc here and throughout), 9 dc in ring; join with sl st in top of beginning ch—10 dc.

Round 2 Ch 3, dc in same st as join, 2 dc in each dc around; join with sl st in top of beginning ch—20 dc.

Round 3 Ch 3, 2 dc in next dc, [dc in next dc, 2 dc in next dc] 9 times; join with sl st in top of beginning ch—30 dc.

Round 4 Ch 3, dc in next dc, 2 dc in next dc, [dc in next 2 dc, 2 dc in next dc] 9 times; join with sl st in top of beginning ch—40 dc.

Round 5 Ch 3, dc in next 2 dc, 2 dc in next dc, [dc in next 3 dc, 2 dc in next dc] 9 times; join with sl st in top of beginning ch—50 dc.

Toddler and Child sizes only

Round 6 Ch 3, dc in next 3 dc, 2 dc in next dc, [dc in next 4 dc, 2 dc in next dc] 9 times; join with sl st in top of beginning ch—60 dc.

Child size only

Round 7 Ch 3, dc in next 4 dc, 2 dc in next dc, [dc in next 5 dc, 2 dc in next dc] 9 times; dc in next 4 dc—70 dc.

All sizes

Rounds 6 (7, 8)–9 (10, 11) Ch 3, dc in each dc around; join with sl st in top of beginning ch—50 (60, 70) dc.

Round 10 (11, 12) Ch 2 (counts as hdc here and throughout), sk next st, hdc in next st (beginning ch and following hdc count as first V-st decrease), ch 1, *V-st decrease, ch 1; repeat from * around, working 2nd leg of last V-st decrease in top of beginning ch; join with sl st in top of beginning ch—25 (30, 35) V-st decreases.

NOTE: *In the following rounds, the legs of the V-sts are worked into the ch-1 sps, skipping the V-sts between ch-1 sps.*

Round 11 (12, 13) With B, repeat Round 10 (11, 12).

Round 12 (13, 14) With A, repeat Round 10 (11, 12).

Round 13 (14, 15) With B, repeat Round 10 (11, 12).

Round 14 (15, 16) Ch 1, 2 sc in each ch-1 sp around; join with sl st in first sc—50 (60, 70) sc. Fasten off and weave in all ends.

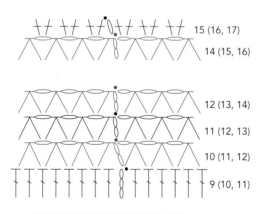

15 (16, 17)
14 (15, 16)

12 (13, 14)
11 (12, 13)
10 (11, 12)
9 (10, 11)

REDUCED SAMPLE OF BEANIE BRIM

STITCH KEY

⌒ = chain (ch)

• = slip st (sl st)

+ = single crochet (sc)

⊤ = double crochet (dc)

⋀ = V-st decrease

Bonnet

Work as for Beanie through Round 4 (5, 6)—40 (50, 60) dc.

Baby size only

Row 5 Ch 3, dc in next 2 dc, 2 dc in next dc, [dc in next 3 dc, 2 dc in next dc] 7 times, dc in next 2 dc; leave remaining sts unworked—42 dc.

Toddler size only

Row 6 Ch 3, dc in next 3 dc, 2 dc in next dc, [dc in next 4 dc, 2 dc in next dc] 7 times, dc in next 2 dc; leave remaining sts unworked—50 dc.

Child size only

Row 7 Ch 3, dc in next 4 dc, 2 dc in next dc, [dc in next 5 dc, 2 dc in next dc] 7 times, dc in next 4 dc; leave remaining sts unworked—60 dc.

All sizes

NOTE: *From here, the bonnet is worked back and forth in rows, to form the top and sides of the bonnet. Turn the work at the beginning of each row.*

Rows 1–4 (4, 5) Ch 3, turn, dc in each dc across—42 (50, 60) dc.

Row 5 (5, 6) (RS) Ch 2 (counts as hdc here and throughout), turn, hdc in next st, ch 1, *V-st decrease, ch 1; repeat from * across to last 2 dc, V-st decrease, ch 21 (23, 27) (for strap)—20 (24, 29) V-st decreases, 4 hdc, and 21 (23, 27) ch. Fasten off.

NOTE: *In the following rows, the legs of the V-sts are worked into the ch-1 sps, skipping the V-sts between ch-1 sps.*

Row 6 (6, 7) With RS facing, join B with sl st in top of beginning ch of Row 5 (5, 6), ch 2, sk next hdc, hdc in next ch-1 sp, ch 1, *V-st decrease, ch 1; repeat from * across all sts (including strap chains) to last 2 ch, hdc in same sp as last V-st decrease made, sk next hdc, hdc in last ch; change to A in last st—29 (34, 41) V-st decreases and 4 hdc.

Row 7 (7, 8) With A, ch 2, turn, sk next hdc, hdc in first ch-1 sp, ch 1, *V-st decrease, ch 1; repeat from * across working 2nd leg of last V-st in last ch-1 sp, hdc in same sp as last V-st decrease made, sk next hdc, hdc in last hdc; change to C in last st—29 (34, 41) V-st decreases and 4 hdc.

Row 8 (8, 9) With C, repeat Row 7 (7, 8); change to A in last st.

Row 9 (9, 10) With A, repeat Row 7 (7, 8).

EDGING
With RS facing, join A in the first hdc of Row 9 (9, 10), ch 1, work 2 sc in each ch-1 sp across front (zigzag) edge and strap. Work button loop across short edge of strap as follows: work 6 sc across short edge of strap, ch 4, turn, sk 4 sc just made, sl st in next sc, turn, sc in each ch across; continue working sc evenly spaced around opposite edge of strap and bottom edge of bonnet; join with sl st in first sc.

FINISHING
Sew the button to the bonnet on the front edge opposite of the strap.

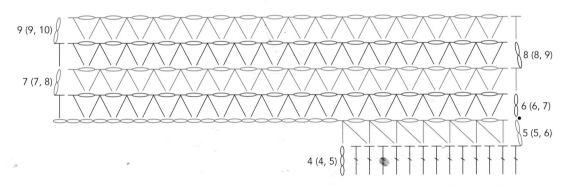

REDUCED SAMPLE OF BONNET STRAP

STITCH KEY

⬯ = chain (ch)

• = slip st (sl st)

⊤ = half double crochet (hdc)

⊤ = double crochet (dc)

⋀ = V-st decrease

everyday washcloths

These subtly textured washcloths make bath time special—splurge on organic cotton yarns to pamper baby's sensitive skin. Worked in a lighter-than-worsted-weight yarn, the crochet stitches form a pliable fabric that's soft to the touch.

SKILL LEVEL
Easy

SIZE	one size
FINISHED CHECKERBOARD CLOTH	8" (20.5cm) square
FINISHED V-STITCH CLOTH	8¼" (21cm) square
COLORS A, B, AND C (checkerboard cloth)	60 yd (55m) each
COLOR B (V-Stitch cloth)	20 yd (18m)
COLOR D (V-Stitch cloth)	100 yd (91m)

MATERIALS
300 yards (457m) of DK-weight yarn: 1 skein each of Sublime *Organic Cotton*, 100% organic cotton, 120 yards (110m), 1¾ oz (50g), in #96 Bone (A), #91 Peapod (B), #92 Borage (C), and #94 Scrumble (D) (3)

Size F-5 (3.75mm) crochet hook, *or size to obtain gauge*

Yarn needle

GAUGE
20 sts and 8 rows = 4" (10cm) over checkerboard washcloth pattern;

8½ V-stitches and 17 rows = 4" (10cm) over V-stitch washcloth pattern.

INSTRUCTIONS

Checkerboard Washcloth

NOTE: *Work this washcloth with three colors of yarn to eliminate weaving in a lot of ends. To change colors, drop color A at the last yarn over of the last stitch of the row and pick up the color B. Work the color B row to the last yarn over of the last stitch of the row and pick up color C on the opposite side. Continue working back and forth, picking up colors at each side, and you'll only have six ends to weave in.*

With A, ch 37.

Row 1 (WS) Sc in 2nd ch from hook and each ch across—36 sc.

Row 2 (RS) Ch 3 (counts as first dc here and throughout), turn, dc in next 3 sc, *ch 4, sk next 4 sc, dc in next 4 sc; repeat from * across—20 dc and 4 ch-4 sps.

Row 3 With B, ch 4, turn, sk first 4 dc; working over ch-4, dc in 4 skipped sts 2 rows below, *ch 4, sk next 4 dc; working over ch-4, dc in 4 skipped sts 2 rows below; repeat from * across to last 4 sts, ch 4, sk next 3 dc, sl st in top of turning ch.

Row 4 With C, ch 3, turn; working over ch-4, dc in 3 skipped sts 2 rows below, *ch 4, sk next 4 dc; working over ch-4, dc in 4 skipped sts 2 rows below; repeat from * across.

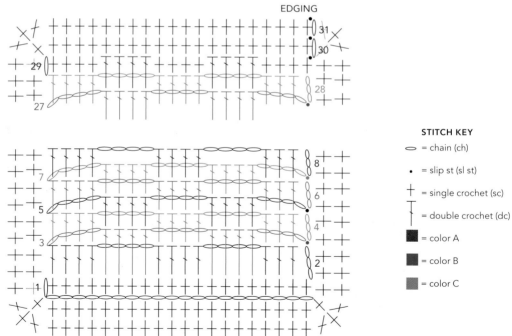

EDGING

STITCH KEY

◯ = chain (ch)

• = slip st (sl st)

╪ = single crochet (sc)

╤ = double crochet (dc)

■ = color A

■ = color B

■ = color C

REDUCED SAMPLE OF CHECKERBOARD WASHCLOTH PATTERN

Rows 5–28 Repeat Rows 3 and 4 and continue changing colors at the end of each row, working 1 row with A, 1 row with B, and 1 row with C.

Row 29 (WS) With A, ch 1, turn, sc in next 4 dc; *working over ch-4, dc in 4 skipped sts 2 rows below; sc in next 4 dc; repeat from * across—16 dc and 20 sc. Do not fasten off. Work edging with A.

EDGING

Round 30 Ch 1, turn, work 132 sc evenly spaced around entire outside edge of washcloth, working 3 sc in each corner; join with sl st in first sc—132 sc.

Round 31 Ch 1, sc in each sc around, working 3 sc in each corner—140 sc.

Fasten off and weave in all ends.

V-Stitch Washcloth

With D, ch 51.

Row 1 (RS) Ch 1, sc in 2nd ch from hook, sk next ch, (sc, ch 2, sc) in next ch (V-stitch made), *sk next 2 ch, (sc, ch 2, sc) in next ch; repeat from * across to last 2 ch, sk next ch, sc in last ch—16 V-sts.

Rows 2–31 Ch 1, turn, sc in first sc, (sc, ch 2 sc) in each ch-2 sp across, sc in last sc.

Row 32 Ch 1, turn, sc in first sc, ch 1, sc in next ch-2 sp, *ch 2, sc in next ch-2 sp; repeat from * across to last sc, ch 1, sc in last sc—18 sc. Fasten off.

EDGING

Round 33 With RS facing, join B in upper right corner; ch 1, work one V-stitch in each sc across; work one V-stitch in the end of every other row across side of cloth; work one V-stitch in base of first sc and each V-stitch across opposite side of foundation ch, V-stitch in base of last sc; work one V-stitch in the end of every other row across remaining side of cloth; join with sl st in first sc—66 V-sts. Fasten off and weave in all ends.

TIP Use these patterns to make burp cloths. Begin working as for the washcloth, but continue crocheting in the pattern stitch until your piece measures 18" (46cm), then follow the directions for the edging, working as many stitches as needed. You'll need about 270 yards (247m) of yarn to make a V-stitch burp cloth and 405 yards (370m) to make a checkerboard cloth.

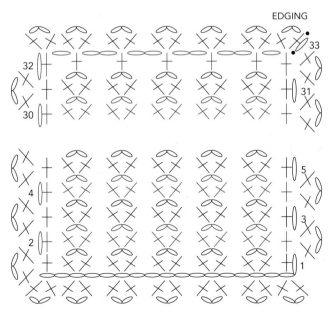

EDGING

STITCH KEY

⬯ = chain (ch)

• = slip st (sl st)

+ = single crochet (sc)

REDUCED SAMPLE OF V-STITCH WASHCLOTH PATTERN

SOFT OWL PILLOW

This oversized pillow is really cute and fun to snuggle—it's sure to delight anyone who walks into the nursery. It's also a great way to use up your worsted-weight scraps—you can change colors as frequently as you like, or stick to the wide stripes as written in the pattern. You'll actually be crocheting a pillow case; a hidden zipper makes the owl-shaped cover easy to remove and launder as needed. Simple instructions for sewing your own owl-shaped pillow form are also included.

SKILL LEVEL
Easy

SIZE	one size
FINISHED MEASUREMENTS (stuffed)	17" (43cm) tall x 14" (35.5cm) wide
COLOR A	180 yd (165m)
COLOR B	220 yd (201m)
COLORS C AND D	130 yd (119m) each
COLORS E AND F	50 yd (46m) each

MATERIALS
760 yards (695m) of worsted-weight yarn: 1 skein each of Cascade Yarns *220 Superwash*, 100% superwash wool, 220 yards (201m), 3½ oz (100g), #810 teal (A), #819 brown (B), #906 green (C), #824 pale yellow (D), #871 white (E), and #877 gold (F) 🔵

Size F-5 (3.75mm) crochet hook, *or size to obtain gauge*

Yarn needle

Straight pins

⅔ yard (0.6m) cotton fabric, 44" (112cm) wide

22" (56cm) zipper

Tailor's chalk

Scissors

Sewing machine (optional)

Sewing needle and thread to match yarn colors

Polyester stuffing or wool roving, about 20 oz (567g)

GAUGE
17 sts and 9 rows = 4" (10cm) over double crochet.

> **TIP** For easy laundering, be sure to use a washable yarn, such as superwash wool (shown), cotton, or an acrylic blend.

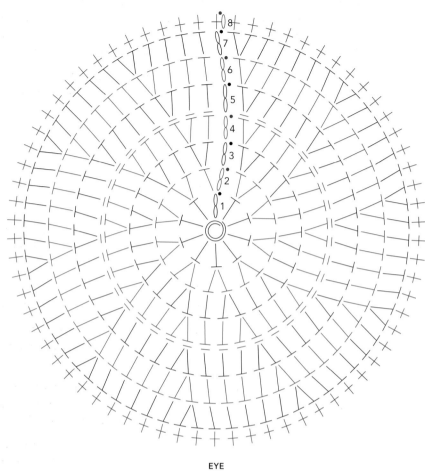

8
7
6
5
4
3
2
1

EYE

EDGING
8

7

6

5

4

3

2

1

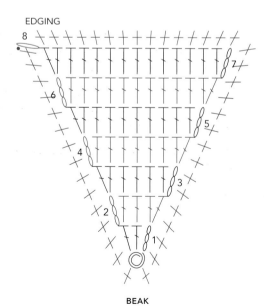

BEAK

STITCH KEY

⬭ = chain (ch)

• = slip st (sl st)

+ = single crochet (sc)

T = half double crochet (hdc)

⊺ = double crochet (dc)

— = worked in back loop only

◎ = adjustable ring

INSTRUCTIONS

NOTE: *This pillow can be finished with or without a zipper. Turn to page 135 to read alternate finishing instructions before completing Round 40.*

Body

With A, ch 33.

Round 1 (RS) 5 dc in 4th ch from hook (beginning ch counts as first dc), dc in next 28 ch, 6 dc in next ch, turn to work the opposite side of the foundation row, dc in next 28 ch, join with sl st in top of beginning ch—68 dc.

Round 2 Ch 3 (counts as dc here and throughout), dc in first dc, 2 dc in next 5 dc, dc in next 28 dc, 2 dc in next 6 dc, dc in remaining 28 dc; join with sl st in top of beginning ch—80 dc.

Round 3 Ch 3, 2 dc in next dc, [dc in next dc, 2 dc in next dc] 5 times, dc in next 28 dc, [dc in next dc, 2 dc in next dc] 6 times, dc in remaining 28 dc; join with sl st in top of beginning ch—92 dc.

Round 4 Ch 3, dc in next dc, 2 dc in next dc, [dc in next 2 dc, 2 dc in next dc] 5 times, dc in next 28 dc, [dc in next 2 dc, 2 dc in next dc] 6 times, dc in remaining 28 dc; join with sl st in top of beginning ch—104 dc.

Round 5 Ch 3, dc in next 5 dc, 2 dc in next dc, *dc in next 3 dc, 2 dc in next dc; repeat from * around, dc in remaining 5 dc; join with sl st in top of beginning ch—128 dc.

Rounds 6–12 Ch 3, dc in each dc around; join with sl st in top of beginning ch. Fasten off A.

Rounds 13–20 With B, repeat Round 6. Fasten off B.

Rounds 21–26 With C, repeat Round 6. Fasten off C.

Rounds 27–34 With D, repeat Round 6. Fasten off D.

Count 13 sts to the right of join, place marker.

Round 35 Join B in marked stitch, ch 1, sc in same stitch, sc in next 5 dc, hdc in next 6 dc, dc in next 40 dc, hdc in next 6 dc, sc in next 12 dc, hdc in next 6 dc, dc in next 40 dc, hdc in next 6 dc, sc in remaining 6 dc; join with sl st in first sc—24 sc, 24 hdc, and 80 dc.

Rounds 36–39 Ch 1, sc in first 6 sc, hdc in next 6 hdc, dc in next 40 dc, hdc in next 6 hdc, sc in next 12 sc, hdc in next 6 hdc, dc in next 40 dc, hdc in next 6 hdc, sc in remaining 6 sc; join with sl st in first sc.

Round 40 Sk first 2 sts, 4 dc in next st (shell made), sk next st, *sl st in next st, sk next st, 4 dc in next st, sk next st; repeat from * around; join with sl st in first sc of previous round—32 shells.

Fasten off.

Eyes (make 2)

With B, make an adjustable ring.

Round 1 (RS) Ch 2 (counts as first hdc here and throughout), 9 hdc in ring; join with sl st in top of beginning ch—10 hdc.

Round 2 Ch 2, hdc in same st as join, 2 hdc in each hdc around; join with sl st in top of beginning ch—20 hdc.

Round 3 Ch 2, 2 hdc in next hdc, [hdc in next hdc, 2 hdc in next hdc] 9 times; join with sl st in top of beginning ch—30 hdc.

Round 4 Ch 2, hdc in next hdc, 2 hdc in next hdc, [hdc in next 2 hdc, 2 hdc in next hdc] 9 times, join with sl st in top of beginning ch—40 hdc. Fasten off B.

Round 5 With A, ch 2, working in back loops only, hdc in next 2 hdc, 2 hdc in next hdc, [hdc in next 3 hdc, 2 hdc in next hdc] 9 times; join with a sl st in beginning ch—50 hdc. Fasten off A.

Round 6 With E, ch 2, hdc in next 3 hdc, 2 hdc in next hdc, [hdc in next 4 hdc, 2 hdc in next hdc] 9 times; join with sl st in beginning ch—60 hdc.

Round 7 Ch 2, hdc in next 4 hdc, 2 hdc in next hdc, [hdc in next 5 hdc, 2 hdc in next hdc] 9 times; join with sl st in beginning ch—70 hdc.

Round 8 Ch 1, sc in each hdc around; join with sl st in first sc—70 sc.

Fasten off.

Beak

With F, make an adjustable ring.

Row 1 (RS) Ch 3, 2 dc in ring—3 dc.

Row 2 (WS) Ch 3, turn, dc in first dc, dc in next dc, 2 dc in last dc—5 dc.

Row 3 Ch 3, turn, dc in first dc, dc in each dc across to last dc, 2 dc in last dc—7 dc.

Rows 4–6 Repeat Row 3—13 dc.

Row 7 (RS) Repeat Row 3—15 dc.

Round 8 (RS) Do not turn, ch 1, work 45 sc evenly around entire edge of beak; join with sl st in first sc—45 sc.

Fasten off.

ATTACH EYES AND BEAK

Referring to the photograph, position the eyes and beak on the front of the crocheted owl and pin them in place. Using B for eyes and F for beak, slip stitch through both the pillow and eye or beak to attach the features (Surface Slip Stitch, page 151).

Sew the Pillow Form

Fold your fabric in half widthwise and lay it out on a flat surface. Flatten the crocheted owl, aligning the shells along the top edge, and lay it on top of the fabric. With tailor's chalk draw a line 1" (2.5cm) from the outside edge, all around the owl. Draw another line following the top edge only of the owl, about 1" (2.5cm) below the first line, and erase (or disregard) the original top line.

Cut out the owl shape through both layers of fabric. Pin the two fabric pieces together with the wrong sides facing. Leaving a ½" (1.5cm) seam allowance, sew all around the fabric leaving an 8" (20.5cm) opening on one of the straight sides. Turn the pillow form inside out and press it, turning the open edges under ½" (1.5cm). Stuff the pillow form firmly, then hand sew the open edges shut.

Finishing

Weave in all ends. Sew one side of the zipper to the inside front edge of the crocheted owl as follows: pin the zipper in place just below the row of crocheted shells and hand stitch the zipper to the case. Repeat for the other side of the zipper, aligning the zipper with the row below the shells on the opposite edge of the inside of the owl. Open the zipper as needed in order to sew it in place. Insert the pillow form into the crocheted owl and zip up the zipper.

ALTERNATE FINISHING: NO ZIPPER VARIATION

If you'd rather not insert a zipper, fasten off after Round 39. Place the completed pillow form inside the crocheted owl and pin the two edges (front and back) together over the top of the pillow form. Follow these instructions to close and accent the pillow.

Row 40 (WS) Working through both thicknesses, with back side of pillow facing you, join B with sc in the first stitch. Removing pins as you go, evenly work 63 more sc across the top of the pillow—64 sc.

Row 41 (RS) Turn, sk first st, *4 dc in next st (shell made), sk next st, sl st in next st, sk next st; repeat from * across—16 shells.

Fasten off and weave in all ends.

TRY THIS!

Substitute Cascade *220 Superwash* in #807 magenta (A), #819 brown (B), #877 gold (C) and #829 pink (D). Substitute color #822 burnt orange (F) for the beak.

TEGUE'S JINGLE BALL

Texture, color, and sound combine in this vibrant toy designed to appeal to baby's senses. Choose high-contrast colors and tuck a few jingle bells inside the ball for maximum fun during playtime. The entire ball is worked in a very tight gauge so that none of the stuffing will escape. I designed this toy for my nephew, Tegue, when he was six months old, and he still plays with it today!

SKILL LEVEL
Intermediate

SIZE	one size
FINISHED MEASUREMENTS	7¾" (20cm) in diameter and 24" (61cm) in circumference
COLORS A, B, C, D, AND E	100 yd (91m) each

MATERIALS
500 yards (457m) of DK-weight yarn: 1 skein each of Red Heart *Designer Sport*, 100% acrylic, 279 yards (255m), 3 oz (85g), 1 skein each in #3529 Grape (A), #3620 Celadon (B), #3515 Lagoon (C), #3570 Iced Violet (D), and #3650 Pistachio (E) **(3)**

Size F-5 (3.75mm) crochet hook, *or size to obtain gauge*

Yarn needle

Polyester stuffing or wool roving, about 10 oz (284g)

6 jingle bells, three 1½" (3.8cm) diameter and three ⅜" (10mm) diameter

GAUGE
Gauge is not critical for this project, but be sure to keep your tension very tight throughout so that stitches are stiff and will not allow stuffing to pass through the crocheted fabric.

INSTRUCTIONS
NOTES: *The entire ball is worked with 2 strands of yarn held together. For minimal tangling, hold the yarn ends from the inside and outside of the yarn ball together and roll them into a ball. Do this for each color used. If your yarn strands become too tangled as you are working, cut the yarn, tie off the ends on the inside of the ball, then begin again with new strands of yarn.*

Change colors at the end of each round. Work colors in the following sequence throughout: 1 round each with A, B, C, D, and E. Remember to change colors on the last yarn over of the last stitch of the round for the best results.

With 2 strands of A held together, make an adjustable ring.

Round 1 (RS) Ch 3 (counts as dc here and throughout), 9 dc in ring; join with sl st in top of beginning ch—10 dc.

Round 2 Ch 1, sc in first st, 4 dc in next dc (shell made), [sc in next dc, 4 dc in next dc] 4 times; join with sl st in first sc—five 4-dc shells.

Round 3 Ch 3, 2 dc in same sc as join, sk next 2 dc, sc in next dc, sk next dc, [5 dc in next sc (shell made), sk next 2 dc, sc in next dc, sk next dc] 4 times, 2 dc in same sc as beginning ch; join with sl st in top of beginning ch—five 5-dc shells.

Round 4 Ch 1, sc in next dc, 5 dc in next dc, sc in next sc, sk next dc, 5 dc in next dc, [sk next dc, sc in next dc, 5 dc in next dc, sc in next sc, sk next dc, 5 dc in next dc] 4 times; join with sl st in first sc—ten 5-dc shells.

Round 5 Ch 3, 2 dc in same sc as join, sk next 2 dc, sc in next dc, sk next 2 dc, [5 dc in next sc, sk next 2 dc, sc in next dc, sk next 2 dc] 9 times, 2 dc in same sc as beginning ch; join with sl st in top of beginning ch.

Round 6 Ch 1, sc in same st as join, sk next 2 dc, 7 dc in next sc, sk next 2 dc, [sc in next dc, sk next 2 dc, 7 dc in next sc, sk next 2 dc] 9 times; join with sl st in first sc—ten 7-dc shells.

Round 7 Ch 3, 3 dc in same sc as join, sk next 3 dc, sc in next dc, sk next 3 dc, [7 dc in next sc, sk next 3 dc, sc in next dc, sk next 3 dc] 9 times, 3 dc in same sc as beginning ch; join with sl st in top of beginning ch.

Round 8 Ch 1, sc in same st as join, sk next 3 dc, 7 dc in next sc, sk next 3 dc, [sc in next dc, sk next 3 dc, 7 dc in next sc, sk next 3 dc] 9 times; join with sl st in first sc.

Round 9 Ch 3, 3 dc in same sc as join, sk next 3 dc, sc in next dc, sk next 3 dc, [8 dc in next sc, sk next 3 dc, sc in next dc, sk next 3 dc] 9 times, 4 dc in same sc as beginning ch; join with sl st in top of beginning ch—ten 8-dc shells.

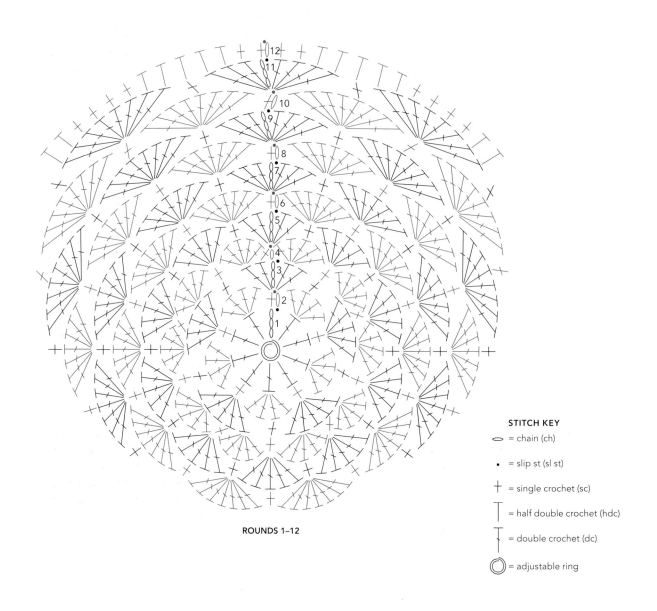

ROUNDS 1–12

STITCH KEY

⬯ = chain (ch)

• = slip st (sl st)

✛ = single crochet (sc)

⊤ = half double crochet (hdc)

⊤ = double crochet (dc)

◎ = adjustable ring

Round 10 Ch 1, sc in same st as join, sk next 3 dc, 8 dc in next sc, sk next 4 dc, [sc in next dc, sk next 3 dc, 8 dc in next sc, sk next 4 dc] 9 times; join with sl st in first sc.

Round 11 Ch 3, 3 dc in same sc as join, sk next 3 dc, sc in next dc, sk next 4 dc, [8 dc in next sc, sk next 3 dc, sc in next dc, sk next 4 dc] 9 times, 4 dc in same sc as beginning ch; join with sl st in top of beginning ch.

Round 12 Ch 1, sc in same st as join, sc in next st, hdc in next 5 sts, [sc in next 4 sts, hdc in next 5 sts] 9 times, sc in last 2 sts; join with sl st in first sc—40 sc and 50 hdc.

NOTE: *Work in back loops only of stitches in all remaining rounds.*

Rounds 13 and 14 Ch 2 (does not count as a stitch here and throughout), hdc in each st around; join with sl st in first hdc—90 hdc.

Round 15 Ch 2, [hdc2tog, hdc in next 7 sts] 10 times; join with sl st in first st—80 hdc.

Round 16 Repeat Round 13.

Round 17 Ch 2, [hdc2tog, hdc in next 6 sts] 10 times; join with sl st in first st—70 hdc.

Round 18 Repeat Round 13.

Round 19 Ch 2, [hdc2tog, hdc in next 5 sts] 10 times; join with sl st in first st—60 hdc.

Round 20 Repeat Round 13.

Round 21 Ch 2, [hdc2tog, hdc in next 4 sts] 10 times; join with sl st in first st—50 hdc.

NOTE: *Secure all of the loose yarn ends inside the ball by weaving them in or tying them in knots. Pack the ball with stuffing and insert jingle bells into the center of the stuffing. Use as much stuffing as will fit and continue to add stuffing as you complete every few rows to ensure that the ball is firm and round.*

TIP For a gentler jingle, use needle-nose pliers to open up one prong of each larger bell. Place the smaller bells inside the larger bells, then close the bells.

Round 22 Repeat Round 13.

Round 23 Ch 2, [hdc2tog, hdc in next 3 sts] 10 times; join with sl st in first st—40 hdc.

NOTE: *For the remaining rounds, fasten off each color as you complete the round and crochet over the ends, as it will be too difficult to go back and weave in all ends once you've closed the ball.*

Round 24 Repeat Round 13.

Round 25 Ch 2, [hdc2tog, hdc in next 2 sts] 10 times; join with sl st in first st—30 hdc.

Round 26 Ch 2, [hdc2tog, hdc in next st] 10 times; join with sl st in first st—20 hdc.

Round 27 Ch 2, hdc2tog around; join with sl st in first st—10 hdc.

Round 28 Repeat Round 27—5 hdc.

Fasten off, leaving an 8" (20.5cm) tail. Use the tail to sew back and forth across the stitches of the last round, then pull the yarn taut to close up the center. Weave in all ends.

make it mini

To make the smaller version of the jingle ball, follow the same pattern using only one strand of yarn and a size D-3 (3.25mm) crochet hook. I used three colors (in sequence: C, B, and E) instead of five, and only needed about 50 yards (46 m) of yarn per color. The ball measures 6" (15cm) in diameter and 19" (48cm) in circumference.

stripe the giraffe

This banded creature is unlike any you'll find in the wild, as crocheted stripes are substituted for spots of color. Stripe's skinny legs and neck are easy for small hands to hold and hug. He would look extra charming in a multitude of colors, but if you prefer a more traditional giraffe, make the body in a solid color and then use a contrasting yarn to embroider spots.

SKILL LEVEL
Intermediate

SIZE	one size
FINISHED MEASUREMENTS (including ears)	16½" (42cm) tall
COLORS A AND B	100 yd (91m) each

MATERIALS
200 yards (183m) of worsted-weight yarn: 1 skein each of Lion Brand *Cotton Ease*, 50% cotton, 50% acrylic, 207 yards (188m), 3½ oz (100g), #186 Maize (A) and #134 Terra Cotta (B) (4)

Size F-5 (3.75mm) crochet hook, *or size to obtain gauge*

Yarn needle

Polyester stuffing or wool roving

1 yd (.9m) scrap worsted-weight yarn (for eyes)

Embroidery needle

Stitch marker

GAUGE
Gauge is not critical for this project, but be sure to create a tightly crocheted fabric to keep stuffing contained.

INSTRUCTIONS
NOTES: *Make all four legs first, then work the body up to the indicated point. Attach the legs to the body, stuff the body, and continue to work the neck, stuffing it as you go. Once the body is completed, you may want to readjust the leg position slightly by sewing the edge of the legs to the body as desired.*

Pieces are worked in a continuous spiral, do not join rounds and do not turn at the end of rounds. To keep track of your work, mark the end of the round with a stitch marker and move it up at the end of each round. The two colors will not match up at the beginning and end of each round, due to the nature of crocheted colorwork in the round. If you prefer, try staggering your color changes, but always be sure to mark the first stitch of the round (regardless of the color of the stitch).

Back Legs (make 2)
With A, make an adjustable ring.

Round 1 (RS) Ch 1, 6 sc in ring—6 sc.

Round 2 Work 2 sc in each sc around—12 sc.

Round 3 [Sc in next 2 sc, 2 sc in next sc] 4 times; change to B in last st—16 sc.

Rounds 4 and 5 Sc in each sc around; change to A in last st of round 5—16 sc.

Round 6 [Sc2tog, sc in next 6 sc] twice; change to B in last st—14 sc.

Round 7 Sc in each sc around; change to A in last st.

Round 8 [Sc2tog, sc in next 5 sc] twice—12 sc.

Rounds 9 and 10 Sc in each sc around.

Round 11 [Sc2tog, sc in next 4 sc] twice; change to B in last st—10 sc.

Round 12 Sc in each sc around; change to A in last st.

Round 13 Sc in each sc around; change to B in last st.

Rounds 14 and 15 Sc in each sc around; change to A in last st of round 15.

Rounds 16–18 Sc in each sc around; change to B in last st of round 18.

Round 19 [2 sc in next sc, sc in next 4 sc] twice; change to A in last st—12 sc.

Rounds 20 and 21 Sc in each sc around; change to B in last st of round 21.

Rounds 22 and 23 Sc in each sc around.

Round 24 [2 sc in next sc, sc in next 5 sc] twice—14 sc.

NOTE: *Stuff the leg before continuing.*

Round 25 Sc in each sc around.

Round 26 Working in the back loops only, [sc2tog] around—7 sc.

Round 27 [Insert hook in next sc and draw up a loop] 7 times, yarn over and draw through all 8 loops on your hook.

Fasten off.

Front Legs (make 2)

Work through Round 2 as for Back Leg; change to B in last st of Round 2—12 sc.

Round 3 Work as for Round 3 of Back Leg; change to A in last st—16 sc.

Rounds 4–6 Sc in each sc around; change to B in last st of Round 6—16 sc.

Rounds 7–30 Work as for Rounds 4–27 of Back Legs.

Fasten off.

Body

Work through Round 2 as for Back Legs—12 sc.

Round 3 [Sc in next sc, 2 sc in next sc] 6 times—18 sc.

Round 4 [Sc in next 2 sc, 2 sc in next sc] 6 times—24 sc.

Round 5 [Sc in next 3 sc, 2 sc in next sc] 6 times—30 sc.

Round 6 [Sc in next 4 sc, 2 sc in next sc] 6 times—36 sc.

Round 7 [Sc in next 5 sc, 2 sc in next sc] 6 times—42 sc.

Round 8 [Sc in next 6, sc, 2 sc in next sc] 6 times; change to B in last st—48 sc.

Round 9 [Sc in next 7 sc, 2 sc in next sc] 6 times; change to A in last st—54 sc.

Round 10 Sc in each sc around; change to B in last st.

Round 11 [Sc in next 8 sc, 2 sc in next sc] 6 times—60 sc.

Round 12 Sc in each sc around; change to A in last st.

Rounds 13–15 Sc in each sc around; change to B in last st of Round 15.

Rounds 16 Sc in each sc around; change to A in last st.

Rounds 17–19 Sc in each sc around; change to B in last st of Round 19.

Rounds 20 and 21 Sc in each sc around; change to A in last st of Round 21.

SHAPE NECK

Round 22 Sc in first 22 sc, [sc2tog, sc in next 7 sc] 4 times, sc2tog—55 sc.

Round 23 Sc in first 21 sc, [sc2tog, sc in next 6 sc] 4 times, sc2tog; change to B in last st—50 sc.

Round 24 Sc in first 20 sc, [sc2tog, sc in next 5 sc] 4 times, sc2tog—45 sc.

Round 25 Sc in first 19 sc, [sc2tog, sc in next 4 sc] 4 times, sc2tog—40 sc.

Round 26 Sc in first 18 sc, [sc2tog, sc in next 3 sc] 4 times, sc2tog; change to A in last st—35 sc.

Round 27 Sc in first 17 sc, [sc2tog, sc in next 2 sc] 4 times, sc2tog—30 sc.

Round 28 Sc in first 16 sc, [sc2tog, sc in next sc] 4 times, sc2tog—25 sc.

NOTE: *At this point, remove the hook from your work and place a stitch marker in the working loop to keep it from coming loose. Stuff the body and use yarn to sew the legs to the body. Remove the body stuffing so that you can secure the yarn ends inside the body. Re-stuff the body, remove the marker and continue crocheting.*

Round 29 [Sc2tog, sc in 3 sc] 5 times; change to B in last st—20 sc.

Rounds 30 and 31 Sc in each sc around; change to A in last st of Round 31.

Rounds 32–34 Sc in each sc around; change to B in last st of Round 34.

Round 35 Sc in each sc around; change to A in last st.

Round 36 Sc in each sc around; change to B in last st.

Round 37 Sc in each sc around; change to A in last st.

Round 38 [Sc2tog, sc in next 8 sts) twice; change to B in last st—18 sc.

Rounds 39 and 40 Sc in each sc around; change to A in last st of Round 40.

Rounds 41–43 Sc in each sc around; change to B in last st of Round 43.

Round 44 Sc in each sc around; change to A in last st.

Round 45 Sc in each sc around; change to B in last st.

Rounds 46–48 Sc in each sc around; change to A in last st of Round 48.

SHAPE HEAD

Round 49 Sc in first 8 sc, 2 sc in each of next 7 sc, sc in remaining 3 sc—25 sc.

Round 50 Sc in first 10 sc, 2 sc in next 7 sc, sc in remaining 8 sc; change to B in last st—32 sc.

Round 51 Sc in each sc around; change to A in last st.

Round 52 Sc in first 10 sc, [sc2tog, sc in next sc] 5 times, sc2tog, sc in remaining 5 sc—26 sc.

Round 53 Sc in first 10 sc, [sc2tog, sc in next sc] 4 times, sc in remaining 4 sc—22 sc.

Round 54 Sc in each sc around.

Round 55 [Sc in next 3 sc, sc2tog] 4 times, sc in remaining 2 sc; change to B in last st—18 sc.

Round 56 Sc in each sc around.

Round 57 [Sc in next sc, sc2tog] 6 times; change to A in last st—12 sc.

Round 58 [Sc in next sc, sc2tog] 4 times—8 sc.

Round 59 [Sc2tog] around—4 sc.

Fasten off.

Ears and Ossicones (make 2)

With B, make an adjustable ring.

Round 1 Ch 2, (3 hdc, 2 dc, tr, ch 2, tr, 2 dc, 2 hdc) in ring; join with sl st in top of beginning ch (ear made), ch 7, turn, 4 sc in 2nd ch from hook, sl st in remaining 5 ch (ossicone made).

Fasten off, leaving an 8" (20.5cm) tail for sewing.

Nose

With A, make an adjustable ring. Work the nose in a continuous spiral and do not join rounds.

Round 1 Ch 1, 6 sc in ring—6 sc.

Round 2 Work 2 sc in each sc around—12 sc.

Rounds 3 and 4 Sc in each sc around.

Fasten off, leaving an 8" (20.5cm) tail for sewing.

Finishing

Sew the ears and ossicones to the top of the head using the long yarn tails.

Whipstitch the nose to the front of the face, leaving a small opening for stuffing (Whipstitch Seam, page 152). Stuff the nose with polyester fiberfill and whipstitch the opening shut. Weave in all ends.

Using a scrap of worsted-weight yarn, embroider a French knot for each eye (instructions opposite).

To make the tail, thread a yarn needle with three 8" (20.5cm) strands of yarn. Pass the needle and first few inches of yarn through one stitch on the back side of the giraffe and remove the needle. Adjust the yarn ends so that both sides hang evenly and braid the strands together for 1½" (3.8cm). Knot the braid and trim the yarn ends.

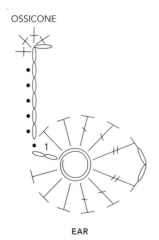

OSSICONE

EAR

STITCH KEY

⌒ = chain (ch)

• = slip st (sl st)

+ = single crochet (sc)

T = half double crochet (hdc)

↟ = double crochet (dc)

↟ = treble crochet

◯ = adjustable ring

How to embroider a French knot

To create the embroidered eyes, thread a needle with yarn and double knot the end. Insert the needle in the space between two stitches on the back of the giraffe's head, bringing the needle out on the RS of the face where you'd like the first eye to be. Wrap the yarn two times around the point of the needle and insert it right next to where the yarn came through the face. To complete the knot, hold the yarn taut and pull the needle through to the wrong side of the face. Bring the needle back out on the RS of the face where the second eye should be and repeat the process (starting at "Wrap the yarn . . .") to make the second eye.

To hide the yarn ends, pull the needle completely through to the back side of the neck via one of the spaces between the crochet stitches. Hold the yarn taut, double knot it, and trim the ends. Use your needle to coax both knotted ends back through to the inside of the head.

TIP To prevent stuffing from coming out through the crochet stitches, line each part with old hosiery. Stuff the hose and tie it off before crocheting the toy part closed.

APPENDIX:
Techniques and stitches

Crochet Basics

Most crochet patterns are worked with a combination of just a few basic stitches. If you are brand new to crochet, these stitches can seem overwhelming, but please be patient with yourself! It takes time and practice to understand how each stitch is made and to crochet at a consistent tension. I'll walk you through the basic stitches with illustrated steps, but I also recommend taking a class or lesson from a friend, because learning is so much easier when someone is available to answer your questions.

With the help of my tech editor, I've attempted to rid the patterns in this book of any right-handed bias. However, due to space considerations, the illustrations in the pages that follow are shown with the hook held in the right hand only. For the purposes of these instructions, think of your "dominant hand" as the hand in which you hold your hook.

HOLDING THE HOOK

There are a couple of different ways to hold the crochet hook—no one way is "correct," so try both and see what works for you.

Method 1: Hold the hook in your hand like a knife, as shown below, using your thumb and forefinger to maneuver the hook.

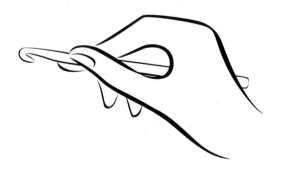

Method 2: Hold the hook in your hand like a pen, working downward into the stitches.

MAKING A SLIPKNOT

Leaving an 8" (20.5cm) tail, wrap the yarn around two of your fingers. Pull a loop of the ball end of the yarn through the wrapped loop and place it on your hook, remove the wrapped loop from your fingers, then tug the yarn ends to tighten the loop.

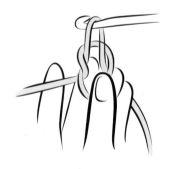

HOLDING THE YARN

Begin by making a slipknot (see above) and placing it on the hook. With your dominant hand, hold the crochet hook so that the ball end of the yarn hangs in front of your non-dominant hand. Make a fist with your non-dominant hand, but leave your pinkie finger extended. Bring this hand toward you and hook the yarn with your pinkie.

Yarn over again and draw the loop through the loop on your hook to make another chain stitch. Repeat this process to make as many chain stitches as the instructions indicate.

Unclench your fist and bring the end of the yarn that's attached to the hook up in front of both your pinkie and two middle fingers, then behind your forefinger. With the hook still in your dominant hand, use your non-dominant thumb and forefinger to hold the bottom of the slipknot already on the hook. As you work, continue to use your non-dominant thumb and forefinger to hold the work. Your tension will be created by the distance between your non-dominant (yarn-holding) forefinger and the crochet hook.

To count chain stitches, hold the chain vertically so that you can see the "V" shapes of the stitches. Count everything but the slipknot and the loop still on the hook as a stitch. There are 5 chain stitches in the illustration below.

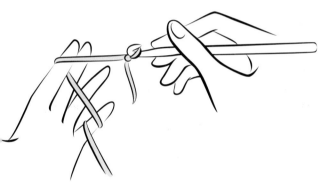

CHAIN STITCH (CH, ⌒)

Begin with a slipknot on your hook. Holding the hook in one hand and the yarn in the other, wrap the yarn over the hook from the back to the front of the hook—this is called a yarn over. Catch the yarn in the throat of the hook and pull it through the slipknot on your hook. Slide the new loop to the shaft of your hook to complete the chain stitch.

SINGLE CROCHET (SC, +)

Insert your hook under both strands of the "V" shape of the 2nd chain from your hook. Yarn over and draw the loop through the stitch.

You now have 2 loops on your hook. Yarn over again and draw the loop through both loops on your hook to complete the single crochet stitch.

HALF DOUBLE CROCHET (HDC, $\top$)

Yarn over and insert the hook under the "V" of the 3rd chain from your hook (skipped chains do not count as a stitch). Yarn over and draw a loop through the stitch.

You now have 3 loops on your hook. Yarn over and draw the yarn through all three loops to complete the half double crochet stitch.

DOUBLE CROCHET (DC, $\top$)

Yarn over and insert the hook under the "V" of the 4th chain from your hook (3 skipped chains count as the first stitch). Yarn over again and draw the loop through the stitch.

You now have three loops on your hook. Yarn over and draw the yarn through the first two loops on your hook.

Two loops remain. Yarn over once more and draw the yarn through the last two loops on your hook to complete the double crochet stitch.

TREBLE CROCHET (TR, ⌐)

Yarn over twice and insert your hook under the "V" of the fifth chain from your hook (4 skipped chains count as the first stitch). Yarn over again and draw the loop through the stitch.

You now have four loops on your hook. (Yarn over and draw a loop through the first two loops—3 loops remain. Yarn over and draw a loop through the next two loops—now 2 loops remain. Yarn over once more and draw the loop through the 2 loops on your hook to complete the treble crochet stitch.

SLIP STITCH (SL ST, •)

Insert the hook under the "V" in the second chain from your hook, or into the indicated stitch. Yarn over and draw the loop through the stitch and the loop on your hook to complete the slip stitch. Slip stitches are used to join rounds of crochet work, or to travel across the work without adding any visible stitches.

WORKING IN THE ROUND

I love to work in the round for one simple reason: Most projects worked in the round don't require working a foundation chain! When you are working in the round, the right side is always facing you (unless indicated) and you don't turn the work after each round—instead, join the round (page 150) to finish it then move right into the next round.

Making a Chain Ring

Forming a ring with crocheted chains is a sturdy way to begin a piece worked in the round. To begin, chain the indicated number of stitches (for example, 4), then join the first and last stitch of the chain with a slip stitch. Work the first round of stitches over the chain ring you just created (rather than into specific chain stitches) unless the pattern indicates otherwise. Once you complete the first round of stitches, pull the tail end of the yarn taut to close up the center of your piece.

Making an Adjustable Ring (◎)

Another way to begin working in the round is to make an adjustable ring, sometimes referred to as a magic ring. To make a ring with your yarn, place the tail end of the yarn behind the ball end, leaving an 8" (20.5cm) tail. With your thumb and forefinger, grasp the yarn where it crosses itself. Insert your hook into the front of the ring and draw a loop of yarn (from the ball end) up through the ring, being careful not to stretch or tighten the ring too much. Holding on to the ring to keep it open, chain the indicated number of stitches, then work your stitches around the original ring. Pull the tail end taut when your first round of work is complete. Adjustable rings are used to start motifs with closed centers, but I don't recommend them for blankets and garments subject to frequent washing, since they can unravel a bit more easily than chain rings.

Joining Rounds

To join the first and last stitch of each crocheted round, work a slip stitch in the first stitch (or beginning chain) of the round you just completed. Do NOT turn the work before proceeding to the next round unless the pattern indicates otherwise. (For complete instructions on working a slip stitch, turn to page 149.)

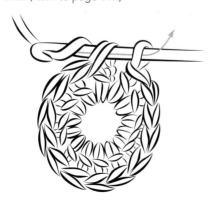

JOINING YARNS AND CHANGING COLORS

In order to join yarn seamlessly in your work, join the new color (or strand) of yarn in the last yarn over of the last stitch made with the old color (or strand). Read it again—it might not make sense at first! To join a new color (or a new ball of yarn) in the middle of a row, work the last stitch with the old yarn up until you reach the last yarn over of that stitch. Make the last yarn over with the new yarn, being sure to leave an 8" (20.5cm) tail, and draw it through the remaining loops on your hook to complete the stitch. Continue crocheting with the new color or strand.

INCREASING

To add stitches to your work, all you need to do is work 2 stitches into the same stitch. In this book, most increases are written into the line-by-line instructions, which clearly state exactly how many stitches to work in each stitch instead of just referring to an increase. For instance, the instructions might say **dc in next 10 dc, <u>2 dc in next dc</u>**. The underlined portion of the instructions is an increase.

DECREASING

To make a decrease, simply crochet two (or more) stitches together. Start by making the first stitch up to the last yarn over, then insert your hook in the next stitch of the row (or round) and work another stitch up to the last yarn over (three loops on hook). This illustration shows how that would look with double crochet stitches.

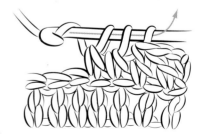

To finish this decrease, yarn over once more, and draw the loop through the remaining loops on your hook.

See also Single Crochet 2 Together, Double Crochet 2 Together, Double Crochet 3 Together, Half Double Crochet 2 Together (below).

FASTENING OFF

When you've finished the last stitch and need to secure your work, cut the yarn from the ball, leaving an 8" (20.5cm) tail. Draw the tail through the last loop on your hook and pull it taut. When you cut your yarn to form the tail, err on the side of a long tail, since there is no way to lengthen a tail that is too short.

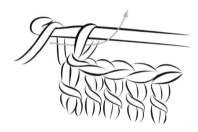

Advanced Stitches

As you work through the book, you might find some stitches that are new to you. Here are some helpful illustrations and stitch definitions to help you along.

SINGLE CROCHET 2 TOGETHER (SC2TOG, ⋏)

(Insert hook in next stitch, yarn over and draw up a loop) twice, yarn over and draw the loop through all three loops on the hook.

HALF DOUBLE CROCHET 2 TOGETHER (HDC2TOG, ⋏)

(Yarn over, insert hook in next stitch and draw up a loop) twice, yarn over and draw the loop through all 5 loops on the hook.

DOUBLE CROCHET 2 TOGETHER (DC2TOG, ⋏)

(Yarn over, insert hook in next stitch, yarn over and draw up a loop, yarn over and draw through 2 loops on the hook) twice. Yarn over and draw the loop through all three loops on hook.

DOUBLE CROCHET 3 TOGETHER (DC3TOG, ⋏)

To make a dc3tog, repeat the part in parentheses for a dc2tog three times, then yarn over and draw the loop through all four loops on hook.

FOUNDATION DOUBLE CROCHET (FDC, ⌡)

Foundation stitches create a foundation chain and the first row of stitches all in the same action. These stitches give the first row of crochet more stretch than a traditional chain.

To work a foundation double crochet, begin by making 3 chain stitches. Yarn over and insert the hook in the back bump under both loops of the "V" in the 3rd chain from your hook as shown, then yarn over and draw up a loop. There will be 3 loops on your hook.

Yarn over and draw a loop through the first loop on your hook—one chain stitch made. Three loops remain on the hook. (Yarn over and draw the loop through two loops on the hook) twice, completing the double crochet stitch as usual.

To make the next stitch, yarn over and insert your hook into the chain you just made, as indicated by the arrow below (illustration shows the four complete foundation double crochet stitches). Yarn over and draw up a loop, yarn over and draw a loop through that loop (chain stitch made), and then make your double crochet in the usual way. Repeat as many times as directed.

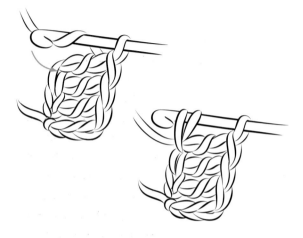

POST STITCHES (FPDC AND BPDC, ⌡⌡)

Post stitches are used to add texture to crocheted fabric. They are made by working a stitch **around the post** of the stitch from the previous row or round instead of into the top of that stitch.

To work a **front post double crochet** (FPdc), insert the hook from the front to the back of the work around the post of the stitch, then back through to the front of the stitch, as shown below. Yarn over and draw the loop around the post of the stitch; you now have 3 loops on your hook. (Yarn over and draw the loop through 2 loops on the hook) twice, completing your double crochet as usual.

To work a **back post double crochet** (BPdc), insert the hook from the back to the front, around the post of the stitch, and back through to the back of the stitch, as shown below. Yarn over and draw the loop around the post of the stitch; you now have 3 loops on your hook. (Yarn over and draw the loop through 2 loops on the hook) twice, completing your double crochet as usual.

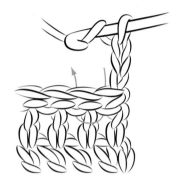

Finishing Techniques

The secret to stellar crochet work lies in the finishing. Neatness counts, so don't hurry through these steps. And remember: If you're working a seam and it just doesn't look right, pull out the last few stitches and try again.

WEAVING IN ENDS

An easy way to weave in your ends is to work over them as you go along. To do this, hold the yarn tail along the top of the stitches you are working into and make your stitches around the tail (to encase it). Work over half of the tail and leave it hanging out so that you can find it later. When you've finished your project, use a yarn needle to weave the tail back through the same stitches you worked over it in the opposite direction, twice. I always weave my ends in at least 3 directions to keep them from working loose, and it's especially important to do this on pieces that will be laundered often and (hopefully) passed down through generations.

BLOCKING

This process remains a mystery to many crocheters, but it's relatively easy and can drastically improve the look of your work. Think of blocking as a way to even out any wonkiness that might exist in your stitches. It can be especially helpful in opening up lace patterns, such as those used in the Sunshine Blanket (page 44) and the Textured Blanket (page 36), and it helps straighten out pieces before they are sewn together (as in any garment, or the Mix and Match Motif Blanket, page 30).

There are a few ways to block, but my favorite is a version of wet blocking. Gather the pieces of your project, a towel large enough to fit the pieces, T-pins, and a spray bottle filled with cool water. Spread your project out over your towel or other blocking surface and spray all of the pieces with water until they are moist, but not drenched. Gently stretch the pieces to the finished dimensions listed at the beginning of each pattern and pin them in place with T-pins. Let the pieces dry overnight.

SURFACE SLIP STITCH

To attach an appliqué (Soft Owl Pillow on page 130) or pocket (Striped Yoke Cardigan, page 72) in a decorative way, try using a surface slip stitch. This seam works best if the piece you wish to attach has a row of stitches around the outer edge so that the edge is crisply defined—if your piece is not already edged, work a row of single crochet stitches around the edge first.

Place the piece you wish to attach on top of the crocheted fabric and pin it in place. Insert your hook under the "V" of any edge stitch on the piece to be attached and through the crocheted fabric. Hold the yarn you are using to make the seam behind these two layers and draw a loop of this yarn through both layers to the front of the work, leaving an 8" (20.5cm) tail behind the work. *Insert the hook under the "V" of the next stitch and through the crocheted fabric, yarn over and draw the loop through both layers and through the loop on your hook. Continue to slip stitch in this manner (repeating the instructions from *) around the entire edge of the piece or as directed.

SLIP STITCH SEAM

For blankets and bulky garments, the slip stitch seam is quick and easy, and most resembles actual crocheting (instead of sewing). This seam will leave a slight ridge on the wrong side of your work, but its advantage is that it's really easy to pull out if you notice you've made a mistake. Use this method for joining several motifs, as in the Mix and Match Motif Blanket (page 30).

Place the two pieces to be joined with their right sides together. Starting at one corner (the right corner, if you're right-handed, the left corner, if left-handed) insert your hook under the "V" of the stitch (or, if you are seaming side edges, into the end of a row) on both the front and back piece. Yarn over and draw a loop through both pieces, leaving an 8" (20.5cm) tail. Insert your hook through the next 2 layers of stitches, yarn over and draw the loop through both layers and the loop on your hook to complete the slip stitch. Continue to slip stitch along the seam.

WHIPSTITCH SEAM

For a sturdy, less bulky seam that lends itself to oddly shaped motifs, try the whipstitch. This seam is visible from the right side of the work, but will blend in if you use yarn that matches the pieces you are sewing together.

Stack the two pieces with their right sides together. Insert a threaded yarn needle from the front to the back through one stitch (or, if you are seaming side edges, into the end of a row) of each of the pieces you are joining. Pull the thread through, being careful to leave an 8" (20.5cm) tail, and then reinsert the needle from the front to the back through the next stitch of both pieces. Pull the yarn through, and again, insert the needle through the next

stitch. Continue in this manner until you reach the end of your seam, then weave in the ends.

MATTRESS STITCH

This seaming method is my favorite for crocheted garments, as it is nearly invisible and doesn't leave much of a ridge on either side of the work. It does take some practice to get it right, so be patient. Use a yarn that matches your project to make this seam truly invisible.

Place the pieces you wish to join side by side with the right sides facing you. Thread a needle and insert it from back to front through the lower corner of the left piece, being sure to leave a tail. Next, insert the needle from back to front in the lower right corner. Insert the yarn in the same way into the next stitch on the left piece, and then into the parallel stitch on the right. Continue in this manner for a few stitches until you see a ladder forming along your seam. Pull the yarn tight every few stitches to bring the pieces together neatly.

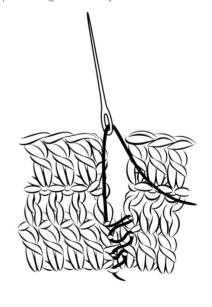

Resources

To find the materials you need to make the projects in this book visit your local yarn shop or craft store. If you need help locating a supplier near you, please contact the distributors listed here.

Yarn

To find a retailer for the specific yarn used in the projects in this book, contact the manufacturer or distributor listed below. While many of the yarns can be ordered online, I can't overemphasize how important it is to see and touch the fibers you are working with, so please pay a visit to your local yarn shop. Employees there can also help you to find a good substitute for discontinued or unavailable yarns. Be sure to buy enough yarn in the same dye lot to complete your project.

Berroco
PO Box 367
14 Elmdale Rd.
Uxbridge, MA 01569
508-278-2527
www.berroco.com

Blue Moon Fiber Arts
56587 Mollenhour Rd.
Scappoose, OR 97056
503-922-3431
www.bluemoonfiberarts.com

Brown Sheep
Company, Inc.
100662 County Rd. 16
Mitchell, NE 69357
800-826-9136
www.brownsheep.com

Caron International
PO Box 222
Washington, NC 27889
800-868-9194
www.caron.com

Cascade Yarns
PO Box 58168
Tukwila, WA 98138
800-548-1048
www.cascadeyarns.com

Coats and Clark
(manufacturer of
Red Heart Yarns)
Attn: Consumer Services
PO Box 12229
Greenville, SC 29612
800-648-1479
www.coatsandclark.com

Classic Elite Yarns
122 Western Ave.
Lowell, MA 01851
978-453-2837
www.classiceliteyarns.com

DMC Corporation
(distributor of DMC
embroidery floss)
77 S. Hackensack Ave.,
Bldg. 10F
South Kearny, NJ 07032
973-589-0606
www.dmc-usa.com

Fiesta Yarns
5401 San Diego Rd. NE
Albuquerque, NM 87113
505-892-5008
www.fiestayarns.com

Knit Picks
13118 NE 4th St.
Vancouver, WA 98684
800-574-1323
www.knitpicks.com

Knitting Fever
(distributor of Debbie Bliss
and Noro yarns)
315 Bayview Ave.
Amityville, NY 11701
800-645-3457
www.knittingfever.com

Lion Brand Yarn Co.
135 Kero Rd.
Carlstadt, New Jersey 07072
800-661-7551
www.lionbrand.com

Lorna's Laces
4229 North Honore St.
Chicago IL 60613
773-935-3803
www.lornaslaces.net

Mountain Colors
PO Box 156
Corvallis MT 59828
406-961-1900
www.mountaincolors.com

Muench Yarns, Inc.
(distributor of Lana
Grossa yarns)
1323 Scott St.
Petaluma, CA 94954
800-733-9276
www.muenchyarns.com

Nashua Handknits
165 Ledge St.
Nashua, NH 03060
800-445-9276
www.nashuaknits.com

Tahki Stacy Charles, Inc.
70-30 80th St.
Building 36
Ridgewood, NY 11385
800-338-9276
www.tahkistacycharles.com

Hooks and Tools

Any craftsperson knows that there's nothing more important than the tools you work with. These three companies manufacture slightly different crochet hooks—I have several of each (eighty-eight hooks and counting!). I particularly love Clover's hooks and tools; their bent-tipped Chibi needles make it so simple to weave in ends and their locking stitch markers help me keep my stitch counts consistent. Susan Bates hooks are pointier than the other brands, so I like to use them for foundation chains. Boye hooks combine the best of both shapes: slightly pointy, but also smooth enough so that the yarn glides well over the hook. Boye also makes a great cushiony grip that fits most standard hooks and takes some of the strain off of your hands. I'm always on the lookout for new tools that make crocheting easier!

Clover Needlecraft, Inc
13438 Alondra Blvd.
Cerritos, CA 90703
800-233-1703
www.clover-usa.com

Susan Bates (Coats & Clark,
See Yarn page 153)

Boye (Simplicity Creative Group)
6050 Dana Way
Antioch, TN   37013
800-545-5740
www.simplicity.com

Blocking Boards

You can find expensive blocking boards in specialty yarn shops, but I use interlocking foam flooring tiles that I bought at Lowe's for less than $20. These tiles take pins readily, allow the water to dry on the surface (instead of absorbing it), and can easily be rearranged to suit any project's dimensions. They also stack neatly when not in use, which means I have more room for yarn! The one thing the floor tiles lack is a grid—if you prefer a surface that is suited both to blocking and measuring, try the traditional padded fabric blocking boards available at Webs.

Lowe's
Lowe's Customer Care
PO Box 1111
North Wilkesboro, NC 28656
800-445-6937
www.lowes.com

Webs
75 Service Center Rd.
Northampton, MA 01060
800-367-932
www.yarn.com

Buttons and Fabric

Add a little something extra to your projects with unique buttons and bright modern fabrics. Major craft stores like Jo-Ann should have a good selection of both, but if you're searching for something more unique, try yarn and sewing specialty shops, or browse through the artisans on Etsy.com. When I lived in New York, I found great buttons and ribbons at M & J Trimming, and pored over the fabric selection at Purl Soho. Luckily, they each have a website for those who can't shop their store in person.

Etsy
55 Washington St., Suite 512
Brooklyn, NY 11201
support@etsy.com
www.etsy.com

Jo-Ann Fabric and Craft Stores
5555 Darrow Rd.
Hudson, Ohio 44236
888-739-4120
www.joann.com

M&J Trimming
Attn: Customer Service Web Department
48 W 38th St.
5th Floor
New York, New York 10018
800-965-8746
www.mjtrim.com

Purl Soho
459 Broome St.
New York NY 10012
800-597-7875
www.purlsoho.com

Helpful Websites

Craft Yarn Council
This is a very helpful resource for information on yarn weight categories, hook sizes, patterns, standard size measurements, and more.
www.yarnstandards.com

YouTube
Search any crochet technique (for instance, your query might be "crochet in back loop only," "half double crochet cluster," or "crochet whipstitch") for a slew of informative videos that will help you along. This is the next best thing to live help!
www.youtube.com

ONLINE CROCHET COMMUNITIES
Crochetville
This site is a friendly forum for crocheters, whether you have a question or want to find someone to crochet a project along with you. The site also offers online classes so that you can improve your skills.
www.crochetville.org

Ravelry
My absolute favorite knitting and crochet website, Ravelry contains a database of every crochet pattern in recent history. This means you can see how different people work the same projects in different yarns and different sizes. I'd love to see your finished projects from this book—upload them to Ravelry and I'm sure to spot them. And add me as a friend, my username is Lindamade.
www.ravelry.com

Other Communities you might like:

Crochet Me
www.crochetme.com

Craftster
www.craftster.org

Further Reading
Barnden, Betty. *Super Finishing Techniques for Crocheters*. New York: St. Martin's Press, 2009.

Crochet patterns are like recipes—I can give you all of the basic ingredients, but how you put it all together is up to you. This book and others like it will teach you how to "cook" with step-by-step how-to photos and tips for professional-looking results.

Chin, Lily. *Lily Chin's Crochet Tips and Tricks*. New York: Potter Craft, 2009.

Pick up years of expertise in just a few hours by reading through professional knitwear designer Lily Chin's insider tips.

Eckman, Edie. *The Crochet Answer Book*. North Adams: Storey Publishing, 2005.

If you find yourself wishing you had someone to answer all of your questions, this book is as close as you can get to a real live expert.

Kooler, Donna. *Encyclopedia of Crochet*. Little Rock: Leisure Arts, 2002.

One of the first crochet books I owned, this is a wonderful resource for both crochet history and stitch patterns. It also contains how-to illustrations for both left- and right-handed crocheters.

Permann, Linda. *Crochet Adorned: Reinvent Your Wardrobe with Crocheted Accents, Embellishments, and Trim*. New York: Potter Craft, 2009.

Check out my first book for lots of cute ideas on accenting the clothes you already own. It's full of quick and simple projects that can be completed in a few hours—perfect if you don't have a lot of time to crochet. Plus, you can add many of the trims and motifs to the little clothes you make from this book!

MAGAZINES
Find more of my patterns and the current work of many talented crochet designers in these publications. I write a crochet Q&A column that appears in each issue of *Crochet Today!*—feel free to submit a question via their website or mine.

Crochet Today!
www.crochettoday.com

Interweave Crochet
www.interweavecrochet.com

acknowledgments

This book was truly a labor of love, and I wouldn't have been able to write it without a little help from my friends. Thanks to my agent Stacey Glick and to Betty Wong, Rebecca Behan, Chi Ling Moy, Jessica Reich, and the rest of the crew at Potter Craft for making it all come together. Thanks also to the super-cute kids who modeled the garments in this book, to Heather Weston for the wonderful photography, and Lana Lê for the book's design. I couldn't do it without my tech editors: Kj Hay, who thoroughly reviewed every stitch and patiently answered all of my questions, and Karen Manthey, who created the stitch diagrams that make these crochet patterns easier to understand.

To all of the generous companies who sent me yarn: Berocco, Blue Moon Fiber Arts, Brown Sheep Company, Caron, Cascade Yarns, Coats and Clark, Fiesta Yarns, Knit Picks, Knitting Fever, Lorna's Laces, Mountain Colors, Muench, Nashua Handknits, and Tahki Stacy Charles, thanks for letting me play, and to Tanis Gray, who helped put me in touch: thank you!

I'll always be grateful to Barbara French and all of the crocheters and knitters at the Bozeman Yarn Shop for opening my eyes to the community a yarn shop can create. And I'm so happy to work with Tammy Rabideau of Yarnivore San Antonio, who helped me stitch the Ribbed Cardigan and constantly entertains my crochet supply stocking requests. To my customers and students: thanks for reminding me why I do what I do!

Thanks also to my friend and fellow author Susan Beal for all of her support, to my sister Ann McNair, for always listening (and for having—and sharing—the cutest kid), and to Paul Heaston, for being my #1 cheerleader and best friend.

Last but not least, to everyone who reads my blog, follows my patterns, takes my classes, and buys my books: **thank you!**

index

Note: Page numbers in *italics* indicate projects.